The Blessings Of Suffering

A Study Of The Book Of Job

B. R. Hicks

Christ Gospel Press
P. O. Box 786
Jeffersonville, Indiana 47131-0786

Publisher: Christ Gospel Press
            P. O Box 786
            Jeffersonville, Indiana 47131-0786

© Christ Gospel Churches Int'l., Inc., 1971

Reedited 2008

ISBN 978-1-58363-005-1

Printed in the United States of America.

Table of Contents

Introduction

Job is the first of the six poetical Books in the Bible. Each Book has a special revelation for us. The Book of Psalms, for example, is a manual of praise and worship; the Book of Proverbs reveals Christ's Wisdom and Humility; the Song of Solomon portrays the love of the Bridegroom for the Bride and the progressive spiritual growth of the Bride; the Book of Ecclesiastes teaches the vanity of the *self;* the Book of Lamentations shows God's great Mercy and Compassion for His people; and the Book of Job reveals the purpose of suffering.

Down through the Ages, people have often wondered why there is so much suffering in the world. Surely, all of us have had problems in our lives that have made us ask, "Why did this happen to me? Why did this suffering cross my pathway? Why am I having to suffer so?" We know God's Word says that man is born unto trouble, but why? Since God gave us the Book of Job to help us understand His reasons for allowing suffering, studying Job's life should be a consolation to us, for in the end, Job confessed God's Justice in putting him in situations of great suffering.

No matter what subject we study in the Bible, we find that all Scripture, from Genesis to Revelation, is laid out in the form of the Cross. A Stature of Truth, portrayed by the four points of the Cross, is used because it pictures the full Stature of Jesus Christ as it is revealed in the Mosaic Tabernacle. The four points of a Stature of Truth depicts the spiritual experiences we will know as we grow to spiritual maturity in Jesus Christ. God is the Master Teacher. He uses figures, types, shadows, parables, metaphors, and allegories throughout His Word in order to illustrate Divine Truth.

When the children of Israel needed a way of approach to and communion with their Holy God in their wilderness journey, God provided the Mosaic Tabernacle, which is a picture, a shadow, a type of the Son of God, the LORD Jesus Christ.

> **Which *was* a figure for the time then present,** in which
> were offered both gifts and sacrifices, that could not
> make him that did the service perfect, as pertaining to
> the conscience; (Hebrews 9:9).

The first Tabernacle, known as the Mosaic Tabernacle, was only a shadow, for that time, of the Stature and Ministry of the second greater and more Perfect Tabernacle, Jesus Christ, Who with Brightness and Glory caused the shadows to flee and the Truth to stand revealed as the illuminating splendor of the noonday sun. The Mosaic Tabernacle was a figure; that is, it was an outlined shape of the Spiritual Stature of Jesus Christ. Thus, four times, God instructed Moses to build the Tabernacle after the pattern that was shown to him in the mount. The seven pieces of furniture in Moses' Tabernacle were laid out in the form of a Cross, with each piece representing a portion of Jesus Christ's Spiritual Stature.

> But **Christ** being come an high priest of good things to
> come, by **a greater and more perfect Tabernacle,** not
> made with hands, that is to say, not of this building;
> (Hebrews 9:11).

The Body or Tabernacle, which the Holy Ghost conceived as He overshadowed the blessed Virgin, was a new fabric, a new order of Building that was infinitely superior to the earthly structure. Since the Mosaic Tabernacle is a divine Blueprint or outline of the Spiritual Stature of the Son of God, it becomes a guiding Light to reveal to our hearts how to grow unto the measure of the Stature of the Fullness of Christ:

> **Till we all come** in the unity of the faith, and of the
> knowledge of the Son of God, unto a perfect man,
> **unto the measure of the stature of the fulness of
> Christ;** (Ephesians 4:13).

6

Because the Mosaic Tabernacle is a picture of the Son of God, in Whom is hid all the Treasures of Wisdom and Knowledge, we may expect the Wisdom and Knowledge of all other Scriptures to fit together with it. The whole Bible is a beautiful revelation of the LORD Jesus Christ. Because of this Truth, God is able to say that ALL Scripture is profitable.

> **All scripture** *is* given by inspiration of God, and *is* **profitable** for doctrine, for reproof, for correction, for instruction in righteousness: That the man of God may be perfect, throughly furnished unto all good works (II Timothy 3:16,17).

Wherever we go in the Word of God, we find Crosses or Statures of Truth. Apart from the Cross of Jesus, we cannot rightly divide the Word of God. The Cross reveals the Full Stature of Jesus Christ.

In this book, which is a study of the Book of Job, Job's character is established in the first chapter. After God has told Satan that Job is perfect, upright, God-fearing, and an eschewer of evil, He allows Satan to test and prove that what He has said about His servant Job is true.

The next three chapters relate Job's experiences with suffering and his final triumph over his pride, which he had not perceived until he had been tried by Satan. Then, the final and fifth chapter tells about the blessings God bestowed on Job that endowed Job with even more than he had in the beginning, before his trials had transpired.

The study of Job's life falls into the following Stature of Truth:

(See stature on following page.)

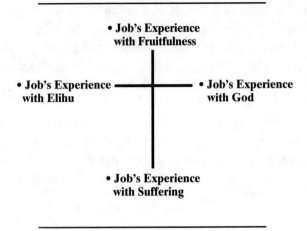

- Job's Experience
  with Fruitfulness

- Job's Experience
  with Elihu

- Job's Experience
  with God

- Job's Experience
  with Suffering

— The Author

Chapter One

Job's Character

What kind of man was Job? Who was Job? As we become acquainted with him, we find that, in his day, Job was a man of note and authority. He lived in the Land of Uz, which was not far from Ur of the Chaldees. Although Job was a man subject to the passions, feelings, and thinkings of all men, he was an unusually spiritual man. Even God acknowledged that Job was a perfect, upright, God-fearing man who eschewed evil. When God called Abram to leave Ur of the Chaldees, He left Job in that part of the world as a witness of the LORD's righteousness. Job's name in Hebrew means hated or persecuted. Job was well named, for his life was characterized by suffering and persecution.

A Stature of Truth about Job's character shows what God thought about him. Surely, here was an exceptional man, one who sought to walk the straight and narrow Way in the LORD's Path of Righteousness and Humility.

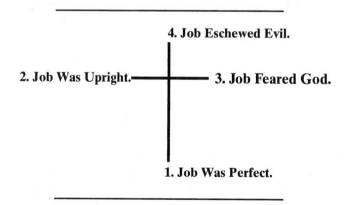

4. Job Eschewed Evil.

2. Job Was Upright. ——————— 3. Job Feared God.

1. Job Was Perfect.

There was **a man in the land of Uz,** whose name *was*
Job; and that man **was perfect and upright, and one
that feared God, and eschewed evil** (Job 1:1).

And the LORD said unto Satan, Hast thou considered
my servant **Job,** that there is none like him in the
earth, **a perfect and an upright man, one that feareth
God, and escheweth evil?** (Job 1:8).

And the Lord said unto Satan, **Hast thou considered
my servant Job, that** *there is* **none like him in the
earth, a perfect and an upright man, one that feareth
God, and escheweth evil?** and still he holdeth fast his
integrity, although thou movedst me against him, to
destroy him without cause (Job 2:3).

I.   Job Was Perfect.

What kind of man was Job? God said that he was perfect. If
this were so, why did God have to put Job in the furnace of affliction and testing? We must understand exactly what God meant
when He said that Job was *perfect.* The word *perfect,* as used in
Scripture, has a twofold meaning: it means full maturity and
growth, but it also means limited perfection. Something can be perfect as far as it has grown or developed. A normal child is not yet
mature, yet he can be perfect as far as he has grown physically. The
Hebrew word that is used in this verse in connection with Job,
indicates that he was perfect as far as he had grown spiritually. Still,
Job had more growing to do before he reached full perfection or a
fully mature spiritual stature. There were new places in God, new
places of faith and love, that Job knew nothing about, but to which
God wanted to take him. Job needed to experience new depths of
humility because he still had much spiritual pride that needed to be
exposed and crucified. In the sense of having attained full spiritual

maturity, Job admitted that he was not perfect, for he said, "If I justify myself, mine own mouth shall condemn me: *if I say, I am perfect, it shall also prove me perverse"* (Job 9:20).

Unless God permits us to go through certain tests and trials, there are areas of our *self*-life, with its imperfections, that never will be brought to light. Only God knows what tests or what particular trials will expose what is hidden deep down in our human heart that is so unlike Him. So much of our *self* needs to be exposed and crucified! We all harbor a secret pride and exalted feelings in view of many different things: our success or position, our good training and appearance, or our natural gifts and abilities, for example. *Self* has an important, independent spirit that makes us stiff and precise in our pride. So many attitudes reveal our pride: our love of human praise; our secret fondness for being noticed; our love of supremacy; our desire to be the center of attention; our feeling of importance when God has anointed us, or when we minister or pray. On the down side, our *self* exhibits anger or impatience which, at its worst, we call nervousness or holy indignation. Our *self* defends its negative attitudes by saying we have a touchy, sensitive spirit. *Self* excuses our resentful or retaliatory disposition when someone else disapproves or contradicts us. All these attitudes need to be taken to Jesus for crucifixion.

Another area of *self* is our *strong self-will* with its stubborn, unteachable spirit; its argumentative, talkative spirit; its harsh sarcastic expressions; its unyielding, headstrong disposition; its driving and demanding spirit; its disposition that loves to be coaxed and humored.

Carnal fear is another great area of the *self.* This part of our *self* is characterized by a man-fearing spirit, a shrinking from reproach and duty, a reasoning that excuses our sufferings as not for our good, a shrinking from doing our whole duty to God before those of wealth and position, a fearfulness that someone will be offended or that our stand for the Truth will drive some prominent person away from us.

Still another great area of *self* is our *jealous disposition;* our secret spirit of envy that we keep shut up in our hearts; the unpleasant sensation we experience in view of the great prosperity and success of another; our disposition to speak of others' faults and failings, rather than extolling the gifts and virtues of those more talented and lauded than ourselves. Our *self* is full of *unbelief* that it expresses by a spirit of discouragement in times of pressure and opposition. Unbelief lacks quietness and confidence in God. Without the roots of belief in God, we have no faith and trust in Him. Unbelief produces worrying and complaining in the midst of pain and poverty and an over-anxious feeling about whether everything, in certain situations directed by God, will come out all right. Another area of *self* that a Christian manifests is formality and deadness, lack of concern for lost souls, dryness and indifference and lack of power with God.

The nature of our *self,* contrasts in an unbecoming way with the Nature of God's Grace. *Self* is crafty; it always likes to show off, while God's Grace is full of simplicity and makes no show of itself. *Self* rebels against crucifixion and subjection, while God's Grace studies self-mortification, resists sensuality, seeks to be in subjection, longs to be subdued, has no desire to use its own liberty, loves discipline, and does not desire to rule.

Self considers what profit it may reap, while God's Grace considers what is profitable to others. *Self* strives for its own advantage, while God's Grace strives for the advantage of others. *Self* willingly receives honour and glory, while God's Grace gives Honour and Glory to God. *Self* fears shame, contempt, and humiliation, while God's Grace rejoices in humility and suffering. *Self* loves leisure and bodily rest, while Grace loves to labor in prayer and the Word of God. *Self* desires and seeks things that are curious and beautiful and abhors cheap and coarse things, while God's Grace delights in simplicity and humility. *Self* respects temporal things, rejoices at earthly gains, and, then, sorrows for the loss of such things and becomes irritated by every slight word or injury, while God's Grace looks to things eternal, cleaves not to the temporal, is not disturbed by losses, and is not soured by hard words.

Self is covetous, receiving more readily than it gives; *self* loves to keep its things private and for itself, while God's Grace is open-hearted, shunning private interests. God's Grace is content with few things. *Self* inclines men's hearts unto the creature and to its own flesh and vanities, while God's Grace draws to God and to His Virtues. God's Grace renounces all creatures and separates itself from the world. *Self* desires outward solace, while God's Grace seeks consolation from the inward Spirit and Word of God. *Self* complains of want, trouble, and pain, while God's Grace endures. *Self* is eager to know secrets and news of this world, while God's Grace is eager to know Jesus Christ and His Word.

God used His great, divine Wisdom in putting Job through the Fire of suffering in order to crucify more of the *self-life* in him and to bring him forth with a greater Spiritual Stature of Grace in his soul.

II.   Job Was Upright.

Job was not like the ordinary man: he was upright, honest, fair, and open in his dealings with others; he was free from deceit and fraud. Job adhered strictly to what was morally and ethically right. Fair, equitable, and of high moral rectitude, Job walked the straight and narrow way — the Crucified Way.

Of all the people on the face of the Earth, Satan chose to attack Job in a special way. Satan's attack should be no shock to us when we start going on for God in the Crucified Way, for it is then that Satan particularly focuses his attention upon us. He is not concerned with lukewarm Christians, for why should he disturb or stir them in any way? Nor does he attack sinners, for he already has his chains upon them. Satan's primary concern is with those who are upright and progressing upward in God, as they crucify their fleshly man and grow in Jesus Christ's Spiritual Stature.

III.   Job Feared God.

Fear is reverence; it is a holy fear toward God. To fear God is to fear displeasing Him. Job walked softly before God, almost quivering, lest he step out of the Way and grieve God. The fear of God that reigned in Job's heart was the spiritual Principle that governed his whole conversation. He had a reverence for God's Majesty, a regard for His Authority, and a dread of His Wrath.

We need to pray that God will give us the kind of heart toward Him that Job had. Often, Christians are more fearful about displeasing their fellowman than they are about displeasing God. Our greatest concern should be to walk softly before Him, in fear of displeasing the One Who gave His Life for us.

How prone we are to take for granted His great Love and Mercy for us, and so we come presumptuously and boldly before Him, forgetting to recognize how great He is and how small we are. When we receive a revelation of Who God really is, we are reduced to proper size and much of our jaunty conceit leaves us.

IV.   Job Eschewed Evil.

To *eschew* means to keep away from something harmful or bad, to shun, to avoid, to abstain from. Job avoided all appearances of sin and approaches to it. With the utmost abhorrence and detestation, he dreaded the thought of doing what was wrong. With a constant care and watchfulness, he eschewed evil.

The words *sin* and *evil* are two different words. *Evil* means misery, affliction, heartache, and sorrow. Job turned his back on evil because he wanted to please God; thus, Job turned his back on anything that would cause misery, heartache, or sorrow.

This, then, is the character of the man called Job. God acknowledged that Job was a perfect man, an upright man, a God-fearing man, and a man who eschewed evil. The unfolding of this man's life, so sorely tried by affliction and loss, enlightens our understanding about the great mystery of why God allows Christians to suffer.

Chapter Two

Job's Experience With Suffering

When we express our desire to the LORD that we sincerely want to progress in our relationship with Him and to grow to maturity in His Spiritual Stature and to become like Jesus, we can well know that it will involve some suffering. Each step that Jesus took in His earthly journey was a step of suffering, and if we are to follow Him, we, too, will walk in suffering.

Other than Jesus Christ Himself, no one in the scriptural records better illustrates human suffering than Job. Suffering is good for all of us because it takes away our shallowness. The details of Job's suffering fits around the four points of the Cross, for he experienced a fourfold suffering.

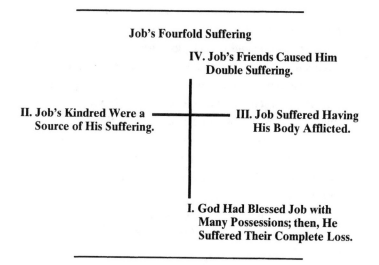

Job's Fourfold Suffering

IV. Job's Friends Caused Him
Double Suffering.

II. Job's Kindred Were a
Source of His Suffering.

III. Job Suffered Having
His Body Afflicted.

I. God Had Blessed Job with
Many Possessions; then, He
Suffered Their Complete Loss.

I. God Had Blessed Job with Many Possessions; then, He Suffered Their Complete Loss.

God's Word tells us that Job's material substance was great and that he was blessed with a large family of seven sons and three daughters. His house being filled with children was an indication of his prosperity. Children are our rich heritage from the LORD, and they are His reward to us (Psalm 127:3-5). The Bible describes Job's substance by numbering his sheep, camels, oxen, and asses. The sheep were named first because they were the most profitable, as King Solomon observed in Proverbs 27:23,25, and 27. Lambs provided wool for clothing, and goats gave milk for food. The account of Job's piety and prosperity comes before the account of his affliction and suffering. God told Job's story in this way to show us that substance, neither physical nor material, will secure us from the common and uncommon calamities of human life.

Job not only looked after his own spiritual welfare but also after his children's welfare.

> And **there were born unto him seven sons and three daughters. His substance also was seven thousand sheep, and three thousand camels, and five hundred yoke of oxen, and five hundred she asses, and a very great household;** so that this man was the greatest of all the men of the east. And **his sons went and feasted** *in their* **houses, every one his day; and sent and called for their three sisters to eat and to drink with them.** And it was so, when the days of *their* feasting were gone about, that **Job sent and sanctified them, and rose up early in the morning, and offered burnt offerings** *according* **to the number of them all: for Job said, It may be that my sons have sinned, and cursed God in their hearts. Thus did Job continually** (Job 1:2-5).

Job offered sacrifices for his children, both to atone for sins of which he feared they had been guilty in the days of their feasting, and to implore, in their behalf, for Mercy to pardon and Grace to prevent the debauching of their minds and to preserve their piety and purity.

A. Satan Came before God to Accuse Job.

Now there was a day when **the sons of God came to present themselves before the LORD, and Satan came also among them** (Job 1:6).

1. Satan Travelled To and Fro and Up and Down in the Earth, Looking for Christians to Accuse before God.

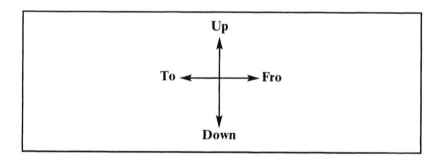

The scene changed abruptly as Satan came before the LORD. The LORD questioned Satan, saying, "Whence comest thou?" Then, Satan answered, "From going TO and FRO in the earth, and from walking UP and DOWN in it." In other words, "LORD, I have been looking for those who are traveling in the Crucified Way of the Cross, those who really mean business and are pressing on in God."

With much subtlety, swiftness, and industry, Satan penetrated into all corners, as it were, of the Cross so that in no place was a person secure from his temptations.

2.   Satan Complained to God about Job.

Then **Satan answered the LORD, and said, Doth Job fear God for nought? Hast not thou made an hedge about him, and about his house, and about all that he hath on every side? thou hast blessed the work of his hands, and his substance is increased in the land** (Job 1:9,10).

Satan complained that God had protected and defended Job's person against him and that God had put a barrier and a guard around Job's house and possessions so that he could not get in to test and try Job.

Satan knew that the LORD had blessed the works of Job's hands. Without God's blessing, although his hands were ever so strong and ever so skillful, Job's work would not have prospered. But with the blessing of the LORD, Job's substance was wonderfully increased. The wicked one saw God's blessing on Job and was grieved at the sight of it. Satan argued that the only reason Job served God was because God had prospered him.

God not only had hedged Job about and had blessed him, but God had increased, multiplied, and enlarged Job's substance in the land. The LORD's blessings had made Job rich. Satan undertook to accuse and to prove that Job was hypocritical and mercenary.

Satan is the accuser of the brethren. When we start out in the Crucified Way, the Way of the Cross, Satan makes his way to the Throne of God and begins to accuse us.

And I heard a loud voice saying in heaven, Now is come salvation, and strength, and the kingdom of our God, and the power of his Christ: for **the accuser of our brethren is cast down, which accused them before our God day and night** (Revelation 12:10).

We may ask, "What kind of God are we serving Who would listen to Satan?" Satan means his accusation for evil, but God takes his attacks and works them out for our good. Satan saw an opportunity to destroy Job, but God looked beyond Satan's eyesight and saw a Fire into which He could put Job that would purify him and bring him forth as pure gold.

Satan accused Job of serving God for a reward. He was saying to God, "Job does not really love you. You have been so good to him and have given him all his possessions, so that is the real reason he serves You. Now, God, if You will take your Hands off of him and let me touch Job's possessions, I will prove to You that Job is serving You only for reward."

We find this spirit in us, for when we are put through the Fire of testing, if we are honest, we find ourselves guilty of serving God for the reward. Many times, in the beginning, if we are ministers, we peach or, if we are laymen, we serve without knowing our real motives. We often are motivated by the desire for a good reputation or for man's pat on the back and his "well done."

Again, God verified Job's commendable character in his walk with the LORD.

> And **the LORD said unto Satan, Hast thou considered my servant Job, that *there* is none like him in the earth,** a perfect and an upright man, one that feareth God, and escheweth evil? (Job 1:8).

Satan continued his accusations against Job, saying, "You, God, have hedged him about and hedged in his possessions." In other words, "Because of your hedge, God, I cannot get to him." This confirms the fact that Almighty God has Satan under His Headship so that before Satan can touch anything that belongs to any of God's children, he must first get God's permission.

What a comfort to realize that regardless of what our tests, trials, or afflictions might be, God permits them and is in control. Never does He allow us to go through trying, dark experiences unnecessarily. Rest assured, suffering is for believers' spiritual welfare; therefore, God's Judgment is Just, Right, and Holy in permitting suffering.

When we tell the LORD that we want to go on with Him, He takes us at our word, and we soon find out if we really mean it or not. We may say, "LORD, I want to learn more about your humility." Yet when He begins to minister but a small portion of humility to us, we begin to complain because we feel greatly abused and misused. As with Job, one of our first tests will be in regard to our earthly possessions. When our possessions begin to suffer loss or destruction, we usually find that we love them far more than we ever realized. It takes a great deal of personal crucifixion before we come to the place in which we are able to rejoice when our possessions are abused and misused in God's service. Jesus allows these kinds of things to happen to us in order to separate our hearts from our possessions; then, we will love Him all the more.

God allows us to suffer so that we can see what is really down inside of us. He wants us to be so in love with Him that we are willing to give up any or all of our possessions if He requires it. We would be unable to love Jesus as much as we do if we knew that He went to the Cross begrudging every step of the way. Knowing His willingness to embrace the Cross makes us love Him all the more and fills us with the sense of our own unworthiness. Yet when God asks us to give up some of our earthly possessions, we feel selfishness rising up within our hearts. We need to remember that Jesus had nothing more to give — He gave His All.

B.   God Allowed Job's Possessions to Be Touched.

In order for Job to receive a true revelation of his inner self, it was necessary for him to enter into a new phase of sufferings. God first gave Satan permission to touch all of Job's possessions.

1.   The Sabeans Destroyed Job's Possessions.

And there came a messenger unto Job, and said, **The oxen were plowing, and the asses feeding** beside them: **And the Sabeans fell *upon them*, and took them away; yea, they**

have slain the servants with the edge of the sword; and I only am escaped alone to tell thee (Job 1:14,15).

Job's first suffering was inflicted by the Sabeans when they took his oxen and asses. God allowed foreign and strange hands to be laid upon Job's possessions so that he might be stripped and humbled, and, thus, brought into greater Knowledge, Wisdom, and Union with God. Job's servants were faithful because the oxen were plowing and the asses were feeding under the watchful eyes of the servants. But all of the servants' prudence, care, and diligence could not prevent the affliction that God had permitted Satan to bring on Job.

God laid His Hand upon Job through the Sabeans. The Book of Job shows the value of spiritual lessons in the Sight of God when man is stripped of his great possessions. In God's estimation, to learn spiritually is the greatest thing one can achieve.

2.   The Fire of God from Heaven Destroyed More of Job's Possessions.

While he *was* yet speaking, there came also another, and said, **The fire of God is fallen from heaven, and hath burned up the sheep, and the servants, and consumed them;** and I only am escaped alone to tell thee (Job 1:16).

The second experience of suffering in regard to his possessions was the destruction of Job's sheep and his servants by Fire that came from Heaven. Greater and greater became Job's suffering; first, the Sabeans and, then, Fire from Heaven destroyed his possessions. This Fire, no doubt, was an extraordinary lightning, and it was leveled so directly against Job that all his sheep and shepherds were consumed at once. Only one was left alive to carry the sad news to Job.

Satan managed this trial very cleverly to try to make Job curse God and renounce his religion by taking away the very sheep that Job sacrificed in honouring and worshipping God.

21

First, Satan had presented Job to God as a false servant; then, he had tried to present God to Job as a hard Taskmaster Who would not protect the flocks out of which he had received so many burnt offerings. Thus, Satan hoped to make Job say, "It is vain to serve God." It is, indeed, a hard test when God allows Satan to touch our possessions with which we worship God.

3.   The Hand of the Chaldeans Destroyed Even More of Job's Possessions.

While he *was* yet speaking, there came also another, and said, **The Chaldeans made out three bands, and fell upon the camels, and have carried them away, yea, and slain the servants with the edge of the sword;** and I only am escaped alone to tell thee (Job 1:17).

The first two messages of destruction had barely been delivered when another servant reported that the Chaldeans had come in three bands to carry away Job's camels and to kill his servants with their swords.

The Fire of suffering burned brighter as Job's possessions continued to be wiped away, but Job stood the test very well, much better than many of us would. If we suffer a little loss of reputation because of men's opinions, we are likely to feel tremendously sorry for ourselves and count this a real suffering. The surrendering of our possessions is a real test of how much we want to press on in the Crucified Way.

Job's possessions were extensive, as Job 1:3 says: "His substance also was seven thousand sheep, and three thousand camels, and five hundred yoke of oxen, and five hundred she asses, and a very great household; so that this man was the greatest of all the men of the east." If God's Fire had fallen upon the wicked robbers, the Sabeans and Chaldeans, God's Judgments would have appeared like great mountains, evident and conspicuous to the most simple babe. But when the wicked prosper and carry off their bounty, while just and faithful servants are suddenly cut off, then it takes a humble, sincere heart to understand the mysterious depths of God's Will and Way. This account gives us a keen insight into the depths to which God will go to perfect a human soul that longs to grow up in His Likeness and Nature.

II.   Job's Kindred Were a Source of His Suffering.

Job, indeed, was not an ordinary man; he walked with God. He showed evidence of spiritual growth and surrender in crucifixion, as it was worked out in him. Sometimes losing one's possessions is easier than losing one's kindred.

God puts man in the Fire of testing to prove what he has learned and to reveal how much growth has taken place in his spiritual life, as well as how much more crucifixion is needed before man's heart and life meet God's requirements.

The Fire of suffering burned brighter as God began to test Job concerning his kindred.

> While he *was* yet speaking, there came also another, and said, **Thy sons and thy daughters *were* eating and drinking wine in their eldest brother's house: And, behold, there came a great wind from the wilderness, and smote the four corners of the house, and it fell upon the young men, and they are dead;** and I only am escaped alone to tell thee (Job 1:18,19).

So Job suffered the death of his seven sons and three daughters. Job's ten children were his dearest and most precious possessions. Our children are part of ourselves and parting with them is very traumatic. To lose them all at once, and for them to be all cut off in one tragic moment, would cut to the most tender part of the human heart, yet Job did not complain as a parent would normally do in these circumstances. He took the Fire of suffering and kept on going in the Crucified Way.

Job even withstood his wife who wanted him to abandon his faith in God.

> **Then said his wife unto him,** Dost thou still retain thine integrity? **curse God, and die.** But he said unto her, Thou speakest as one of the foolish women speaketh. What? shall we receive good at the hand of God, and shall we not receive evil? **In all this did not Job sin with his lips** (Job 2:9,10).

After God had permitted Satan to smite Job's body with sore boils, Job experienced suffering his wife's counsel to "curse God, and die." Oh, the suffering of misunderstanding when our companions are not walking in the Crucified Way! They will jeer and say things like, "So this is where the Crucified Way has brought you."

Job's wife scoffed at her husband's piety. She taunted Job for his constancy to his religion.

Satan makes use of those near and dear to us to tempt us. Adam-male was tempted by Adam-female, and Christ was tempted by Peter. We must, therefore, carefully watch not to be drawn to say or do a wrong thing because of the influence of those near to us.

The Crucified Way is the *Suffering Way.* We will not escape pain and suffering when we go in Jesus' Footsteps. As Jesus suffered, so must His own suffer. We need to be long-suffering as more of our *self* and our flesh, which needs to be crucified, are revealed to us.

A.   Job Reacted to His Suffering in Four Ways.

The following verse describes Job's reaction to his suffering:

> **Then Job** arose, and **rent his mantle,** and **shaved his head,** and **fell down upon the ground,** and **worshipped,** (John 1:20).

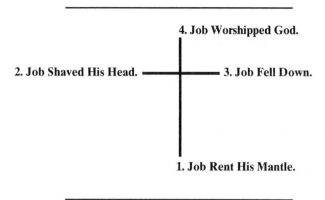

4. Job Worshipped God.

2. Job Shaved His Head. —————|————— 3. Job Fell Down.

1. Job Rent His Mantle.

1.   Job Rent His Mantle.

Job did not heatedly throw off his clothes, but he very gravely rent his mantle — his cloak or outer garment. In Eastern countries, a man's power and authority were revealed by the type of mantle he wore. The mantle was a long garment that was worn around the neck and shoulders; it extended down toward the hem of the outer garment. The longer the mantle, the more power and authority were enjoyed by the individual wearing it.

The Bible says that Job was the greatest man in the East; therefore, beloved, for Job to take off his mantle and rend his garment was a very significant act. Instead of complaining against God, he laid down his own power and authority, as it were, and rent it in two or began to humble himself, which is proven by the next step Job took.

2.   Job Shaved His Head.

Job did not passionately tear his hair but deliberately shaved his head. Shaving his head was a symbol of Job's humbling himself and surrendering his own mind to God's Mind. He humbled himself under God's Hand.

3. Job Fell Down.

Job fell down upon the ground, as low as he could get. He abased himself to the very dust of the Earth, in patient submission to God's Will. Hereby, he showed his sincerity and prepared himself to obtain good from his affliction.

4. Job Worshipped God.

Through Job's suffering, God proved Satan to be a liar. At this time, Job displayed his worship in a fourfold manner.

> And said, **Naked came I out of my mother's womb, and naked shall I return** thither: **the LORD gave, and the LORD hath taken away; blessed be the name of the LORD** (Job 1:21).

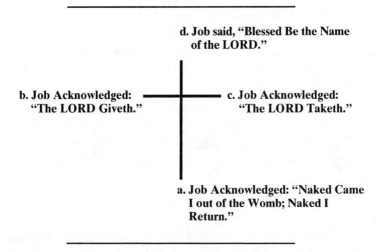

d. Job said, "Blessed Be the Name of the LORD."

b. Job Acknowledged: "The LORD Giveth."

c. Job Acknowledged: "The LORD Taketh."

a. Job Acknowledged: "Naked Came I out of the Womb; Naked I Return."

a. Job Acknowledged: "Naked Came I out of the Womb; Naked I Return."

Job worshipped God by recognizing the Truth of God's Word. Man's origin was dust, and to dust we shall return: "In the sweat of thy face shalt thou eat bread, *till thou return unto the ground; for out of it wast thou taken:* for dust thou art, *and unto dust shalt thou return*" (Genesis 3:19). We, too, can worship God in our sufferings and afflictions if we acknowledge the Truth of His Word. This consideration caused Job to remain silent in spite of all his losses.

b. Job Acknowledged: "The LORD Giveth."

Job worshipped God by acknowledging all his blessings, wealth, increase, and children as being given to him by God's Hand.

c. Job Acknowledged: "The LORD Taketh."

Job did not say, "The LORD gave, and the Sabeans and Chaldeans have taken away; God made me rich, but Satan has made me poor." Instead, he worshipped God in his acknowledgment that the LORD had made him rich and that the LORD also had taken away his possessions.

d. Job Said, "Blessed Be the Name of the LORD."

Job adored God through all his suffering. He blessed the Name or Nature of the LORD. In so doing, he acknowledged God as being Just and Holy in Character and Nature. Afflictions must not divert us from offering praise and worship to God.

Job had to have had a great degree of surrender to God's Headship in order to have worshipped God as he did under his adverse circumstances. Again, he stood the test on his journey in the Crucified Way. "In all this Job sinned not, nor charged God foolishly" (Job 1:22).

God wants us to be so surrendered inside, in our hearts, that whatever happens, we can rejoice and leap for joy.

In his suffering, Job first suffered the loss of his possessions; then, he lost his sons and daughters. His wife caused him to suffer disunity because she did not understand God's plan for Job.

Finally, Satan asked God to let him touch Job's bone and flesh.

III. Job Suffered Having His Body Afflicted.

> **And Satan answered the LORD,** and said, Skin for skin, yea, all that a man hath will he give for his life. But **put forth thine hand now, and touch his bone and his flesh, and he will curse thee to thy face.** And the LORD said unto Satan, Behold, he *is* in thine hand; but save his life. **So went Satan forth** from the presence of the LORD, **and smote Job with sore boils from the sole of his foot unto his crown.** And he took him a potsherd to scrape himself withal; and he sat down among the ashes (Job 2:4-8).

Satan continued pushing ahead in his malicious persecution of Job, whom he hated because God loved him. He did all he could to separate Job from God, as he sought to sow discord and make mischief between them by urging God to afflict Job and, then, by urging Job to blaspheme God. One would have thought that Satan would have ceased when he had been shamefully baffled, disappointed, and proven a liar, but malice is restless and knows no end to its onslaught.

Thus far, Job had passed each successive test, as he walked in the Crucified Way, but the most personal and difficult test came when God gave Satan permission to touch Job's body with sore boils — from the top of his head to the soles of his feet. Some historians contend that Job had a contagious disease similar to leprosy, which meant that he had to go outside the city. Job went outside of the city to the ash heap on the dunghill and sat there scraping his boils with a broken piece of pottery, put there for that purpose. This piece was called a potsherd. (It is marvelous how God provides for our every need.)

The people of the East are very sensitive, even about their broken cooking vessels. When Americans break a clay pot, it is thrown into the garbage can, but this is not true with eastern people.

In past times, their broken pieces were put on the ash heap because they knew that a leper or someone would get a disease and would need something to scrape away the corruption from his body. Also, broken pieces of pottery were placed by a spring, a well, or a stream so that some thirsty, wayfaring traveler could get a drink of water.

The potsherd presents a precious picture of humility. When we become as a broken piece of pottery, God can use us in His service, even if it is only to ease someone's disease, give a drink of water, or a word fitly spoken.

Satan declared to God, "If you touch Job's body, he will curse You to your face." The pressure of testing finally overtook Job, and he poured out murmuring and complaining that he did not know he had within him. So it is with us; in the beginning of suffering, we may get along pretty well, but continuous day and night suffering usually brings out murmurings, unbelief, and other weaknesses we harbor within. Thus, we discover that we need more spiritual growth.

Job's final suffering was brought on by his friends.

IV.   Job's Friends Caused Him Double Suffering.

> Now **when Job's three friends heard of all this evil that was come upon him, they came every one from his own place;** Eliphaz the Temanite, and Bildad the Shuhite, and Zophar the Naamathite: **for they had made an appointment together to come to mourn with him and to comfort him.** And when they lifted up their eyes afar off, and knew him not, they lifted up their voice, and wept; and they rent every one his mantle,

and sprinkled dust upon their heads toward heaven. So they sat down with him upon the ground seven days and seven nights, and none spake a word unto him: for they saw that *his* grief was very great (Job 2:11-13).

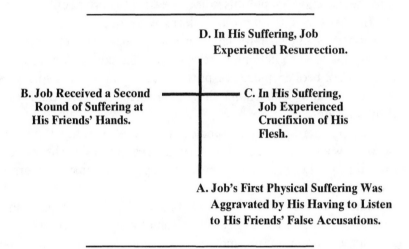

D. In His Suffering, Job Experienced Resurrection.

B. Job Received a Second Round of Suffering at His Friends' Hands.

C. In His Suffering, Job Experienced Crucifixion of His Flesh.

A. Job's First Physical Suffering Was Aggravated by His Having to Listen to His Friends' False Accusations.

The expression *Job's comforters* describes friends who visit a person who is in distress but whose presence, boasting, and advice cause the distressed person added suffering. Job's friends came to see him in their spiritual pride and self-righteousness, thinking that they knew so much about God. But their accusations, bigotry, and pride only caused Job greater suffering.

Job's heart was hot within him, and while he thought on his suffering, his fire of anxiety burned. The extremity of his trouble and the discomposure of his spirit had made him forget the good to which he had been born. He was filled with thoughts of only the evil and wished that he had never been born.

To curse the day of our birth because we have entered upon some calamitous scene of life is to quarrel with the Headship of God and to despise the dignity of our being. However, the promised life hereafter, with the divine consolations to support us in the prospect of it, makes us know that we were not born in vain.

Job's folly and weakness made him curse the day he had been born. Job cursed his day, but he did not curse God. Job was weary of his life, but he was not weary of serving God.

Satan had accused Job of being a hypocrite who secretly hated God and who, if provoked, would show his hatred. But Satan again was proven a liar. Although Job cursed his day of birth, he never cursed God. Because he lacked greater Knowledge and experience in God, Job poured out his fleshly murmurings and complainings; thus, Job's *self* began to be exposed.

Likewise, we, too, occasionally experience a little tongue-lashing from our spouse, our friend, our loved ones, and, in spite of all of our good intentions to keep our mouth shut, we weaken, sooner or later, and curse our day. What day? The day of our birth. In despair, we ask the LORD why we were born into this troublesome world. The answer is obvious: to love the LORD and to press on for God and to thank the LORD for putting us in the Fire of testing so that we might come forth as pure gold.

A. Job's First Physical Suffering Was Aggravated by His Having to Listen to His Friends' False Accusations.

Job would have fared better in his physical suffering had his friends kept silent, but God permitted them to speak, which added to Job's sufferings.

Job's case presents some precious lessons for us to learn about how to treat sick people. When one is suffering, much jabbering, loud speaking, and activity only add to the patient's suffering. People often have the false concept of exercising their fleshly ideas and wisdom of being noisy and boisterous in trying to cheer up the sick, but a sick person needs a gentle, tender, kind comforter. The Holy Ghost can give us a special, powerful anointing to be very vigil and tender and quiet in the presence of a sick person. Another lesson to learn is being able to realize how long to visit with the sick; should we make a brief visit or an extended one?

Job's sufferings with his friends comprise many chapters in the Book of Job. Job's friends mistook spiritual experience for spiritual growth.

At times, God lifts us up above our own spiritual stature of growth into a higher realm, only to bring us down again for further crucifixion so that we might grow up into a higher realm in God. We must not mistake those temporary experiences of exalting vision as indications of our present attainment of spiritual stature. This was what Job's friends did.

While Job was suffering in his body, he began to complain, bemoaning the day he was born and wondering why he, as a babe at his mother's knee, had not given up the ghost right then. During this time, Job's friends silently sat with him for seven days and seven nights without uttering a word. Finally, they broke their silent vigil. A Stature of Truth about Job's friends and their speeches shows their spiritual condition.

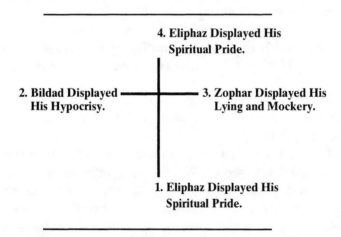

4. Eliphaz Displayed His Spiritual Pride.

2. Bildad Displayed His Hypocrisy.

3. Zophar Displayed His Lying and Mockery.

1. Eliphaz Displayed His Spiritual Pride.

1. Eliphaz Displayed His Spiritual Pride (Job, 4 and 5).

Eliphaz means *god of gold.* He was the leader of Job's comforters and the first one to speak. Eliphaz spoke out of his spiritual pride and his high estimation of himself.

God's Word exhorts us to speak the Truth in love. Love comes as we grow in spiritual stature, and without this degree of spiritual stature, we cannot consistently minister the Truth of God's Word in love unto others.

Eliphaz did not exercise love. Instead, he ministered in the place of a judge, reprimanding Job as though he knew what was wrong with him. It was Eliphaz's opinion that Job was getting exactly what he deserved, and his attitude reflected only disgust and impatience with poor, suffering Job.

> But now **it is come upon thee, and thou faintest; it toucheth thee, and thou art troubled.** *Is* **not** *this* **thy fear, thy confidence, thy hope, and the uprightness of thy ways?**
> (Job 4:5,6).

Eliphaz took notice of Job's former service and ministry to the comfort of others. He acknowledged that Job had instructed many relatives, friends, and neighbors, and that he had strengthened feeble knees. Nevertheless, he charged Job with weakness and faintheartedness in his suffering and affliction. He upbraided Job for his low spiritedness. He made light of Job's affliction, saying, "It *toucheth* thee." These were the very words that Satan himself used in Job 1:11 and Job 2:5. If Eliphaz had felt even half of Job's affliction, he would have said, "It smites thee; it wounds thee; it is killing thee." But, as far as Job's affliction was concerned, Eliphaz considered the affliction only a *touch.* Even though Job fainted in the day of adversity, it was no sign that he was without a measure of the LORD's Strength and Grace.

Job's *friends* were blind to the Crucified Way and unaware that God had put Job into the Fire of testing to purify some of His wrong inner attitudes and dispositions. Job was put in the Fire of testing to reveal his spiritual pride, self-righteousness, and other attitudes of which he was unconscious. Job was an honest and sincere man and was perfect, as far as he had grown in his spiritual development; however, his friends accused him of sowing wickedness and of covering up some secret sin; therefore, in their judgment, he was reaping what he deserved.

Eliphaz continued by telling about his own great experience, which supposedly qualified him to discern Job's trouble. Basing his authority on his one little experience, Eliphaz thought that he had sufficient ability to counsel Job in his dilemma.

> **Now a thing was secretly brought to me, and mine ear received a little thereof. In thoughts from the visions of the night, when deep sleep falleth on men,** Fear came upon me, and trembling, which made all my bones to shake. Then a spirit passed before my face; the hair of my flesh stood up: It stood still, but I could not discern the form thereof: an image *was* before mine eyes, *there was* silence, and I heard a voice, *saying,* Shall mortal man be more just than God? shall a man be more pure than his maker? Behold, he put no trust in his servants; and his angels he charged with folly: How much less *in* them that dwell in houses of clay, whose foundation *is* in the dust, *which* are crushed before the moth? They are destroyed from morning to evening: they perish for ever without any regarding *it.* Doth not their excellency *which is* in them go away? they die, even without wisdom (Job 4:12-21).

Eliphaz had undertaken to convince Job of the sin and folly of his discontent and impatience; then, he related a vision he had received, trying to convince Job that he was able to discern the reason for Job's sufferings.

God was trying to show Eliphaz his *own* need with the experience he had had in his vision. When you have a vision or dream by night, be careful not to pass it off to *someone else* by telling him what is wrong because of your own little experience. Let God work in your own life, for had Eliphaz done this, he would have tasted crucifixion of his own spiritual pride and would have then been able to instruct Job wisely.

In Job, chapter five, Eliphaz prated about things that people know, such as the Truth that God is Great, and He does marvelous and unsearchable things. He still was not assisting Job, only persecuting him by trying to teach Job things he *himself* had not learned. Beloved, God wants us to be shining examples of the Crucified Way in order to teach others and to have victory ourselves.

The Truth was that Eliphaz spoke out of spiritual pride and superiority, thereby mistaking his spiritual experience for great spiritual stature. In fact, he only added to Job's sufferings by increasing his mental torture.

2. Bildad Displayed His Hypocrisy (Job 8, 9, and 10).

The name *Bildad* means *son of contention*. Bildad really was a contender, and his contention heaped up more suffering on Job. He was the second friend to speak to Job, and he accused Job of being a hypocrite, although God had said that Job was a perfect man, as far as he had grown spiritually. A hypocrite is one who is insincere and who puts on an outward form of spirituality, but who is inwardly insincere with God. It is painful enough to be in the Fire of suffering when God is trying us, let alone having someone accuse us of being a hypocrite. It hurts to be called a hypocrite, and Bildad's accusation only added to Job's sufferings.

Most people measure others by the outward appearance of things, and so did Job's friends. They based their estimation of themselves on their outward appearance, their possessions, and their earthly gain. Because someone is not prosperous does not mean that he is not going on for God or vice versa. God knows what is best for our spiritual growth, and, sometimes, He takes away our material or physical prosperity so that we will prosper spiritually. God strips us outwardly in order for us to grow inwardly. Outward prosperity is

not a sign of God's blessing, for were that the case, then God's blessings would sometimes be on sinners more than on His own people.

Job's friends came to the wrong conclusion, for they were basing
their judgment and accusations on Job's outward circumstances, little
realizing that Job was in the furnace of affliction because God had
permitted him to be there. Bildad's spiritual pride, like an eager,
angry disputant, accused Job of knowing nothing.

With our mouths, we say that we are nothing, but just let someone else say that about us and see how quickly we pout and become
offended and angry. Then, we show what we really are like inside.

This was true in Job's case also. He suffered great offense when
his friends reprimanded him as though he knew nothing. In chapters nine and ten, Job tried to defend himself, hoping to receive
comfort, consolation, and consideration.

This was God's very reason for putting Job in the Fire. The
Purpose of God's Fire is to cut us off from all fleshly and human comfort and thereby cause us to look to God for consolation. The same
applies to spiritual parents; God will cut us off from human comfort
and sympathy. The more Job tried to defend and explain, the less sympathy, comfort, and consolation he received.

Later, when Job had learned his lesson and had seen himself for
what he really was, he abhorred himself, repented in sackcloth and
ashes, and humbled himself before God.

When rejected and separated from all human consolation, we
must all learn to turn to Jesus Christ. When we look to Him for comfort, we find that He never fails. What a valuable lesson this is to learn.

3.   Zophar Displayed His Lying and Mockery (Job 11).

The name *Zophar* means *to skip about.* There are those who skip
about and all around a subject, trying to create the impression that
they are very knowledgeable, yet they know nothing.

Zophar was the third friend who spoke to Job. He saw Job as a liar
and a mocker. Eliphaz had begun with a more modest rebuke. He

said, "If we assay to commune with thee, wilt thou be grieved: but who can withhold himself from speaking" (Job 4:2). Bildad was a little rougher. He said, "How long wilt thou speak these things? and how long shalt the words of thy mouth be like a strong wind?" (Job 8:2).

However, Zophar fell upon poor Brother Job without mercy. He asked, "Should not the multitude of words be answered? and should a man full of talk be justified? Should thy lies make men hold their peace? and when thou mockest, shall no man make thee ashamed?" (Job 11:2,3).

After Job, in his suffering, had made a tremendous plea for mercy, understanding, and pity, he received more tongue-lashing from Zophar.

No one can love or sympathize without understanding, and this requires some growth in the Spiritual Stature of Truth. Beloved, only as we love, give, comfort, and minister God's Truth and instruction will others be brought into a place of liberty and freedom through our efforts. Although Job's suffering was great, his present suffering was not worthy to be compared to the fruitfulness that Job experienced after his chastening.

His friends attempted to put Job to shame, but he fought back. They only stirred up his flesh and theirs as well. Flesh begets flesh; *self* begets *self.* Up to this point, Job had been honest, as far as he knew how to be. God was after some things that Job was unaware of in his life. Further cleansing was necessary before God was able to open up a new realm in growth in spiritual stature to Job.

Zophar, like the other friends, had no Knowledge of the Cross Way, the Crucified Way, nor did he know very much about how God searches out and reveals and exposes men's hearts. Zophar detected that Job was hiding some wickedness in his heart, but his ignorance of how to go on with God kept him from reaching the right conclusion. Only God can reveal what is in a man's heart, and even though Zophar detected Job's need, to an extent, he still did not understand what God was doing with Job.

4.   Eliphaz Again Displayed His Spiritual Pride (Job 15).

Eliphaz spoke again. This time, he accused Job not only of pride but of winking at sin — hidden sin. Speaking out of his own pride, Eliphaz saw only that Job was deceitful; whereas, God Himself already had declared Job upright and God-fearing.

Job's friends brought him anything but comfort. Job was like a boxer fighting several opponents in a ring, with each slugging away at him. Before he could regain his senses from one blow, another one punched him with more accusations. These so-called "comforters" made themselves equal with God and placed themselves with the Ancients and called Job a *babe*. All the time, God was permitting this harassment in order to teach Job to look to Him and not to man.

Many people base their Christian experience on hearsay. Traditions of men are hearsay. As long as we have only *heard,* we do not know the facts ourselves; we have only second-hand information. When someone testifies of something real that they have received from God, then we should fall down on our knees, fast and pray, and cling to our Heavenly Father until He makes the matter personally known unto us.

Eliphaz kept needlessly repeating the traditions, rehearsing the fact that the wicked will perish and be consumed by the flame. Job knew this fact better than Eliphaz.

It is futile to give a sinner's message to a saint, especially one who is going on in the Crucified Way. Christians are no longer concerned with the threat of hellfire, but they do need to know what is hindering them from going on for God, and only God can rightly reveal this to them. Still, Eliphaz delighted in tormenting poor Job, as he continued falsely to accuse him of wickedness and sin.

> For **the congregation of hypocrites *shall be* desolate, and fire shall consume the tabernacles of bribery. They conceive mischief, and bring forth vanity, and their belly prepareth deceit** (Job 15:34,35).

In retrospect, we have discussed Job's suffering concerning his possessions, his kindred, and his body. In the Fire, Job's suffering was complete, since it encompassed his spirit, soul, and body. He was racked with pain from the bottom of his feet to the top of his head, and as he was sitting on the ash heap scraping his boils, his friends added *mental* suffering and agony to his *physical* torment.

This ends the first Stature of Truth about Job's suffering. The second Stature of Truth concerning Job's continuing suffering at the hands of his friends is found in chapters eighteen, twenty, twenty-two, and twenty-five of the Book of Job.

B. Job Received a Second Round of Suffering at His Friends' Hands.

In the continuance of Job's suffering, set forth by this second Stature of Truth about his experience with his friends, Job still begged for pity, mercy, and understanding, but he got none. Instead, his friends gave him another bout of inconsiderate, so-called sympathy. Their comments, this second time around, showed that his friends had not changed their opinions of Job nor of the reasons for his suffering.

1. Bildad Accused Job of Being a Sinner (Job18).

In the first Stature of Truth about Job's suffering, Bildad had accused Job of being a hypocrite; this time, he accused him of being a sinner, of not even knowing God. An unbelieving, worldly sinner is a far cry from a believer who is living at the Laver of cleansing and who is letting God dig deeply within his heart to expose his attitudes, dispositions, and motives that are unlike the LORD.

Bildad shot arrows of bitter words at Job, not realizing that he was serving Satan's design in adding affliction to Job. Bildad revealed his own spiritual pride, for he grew weary of hearing others speak and was impatient until his turn came. We ought to be swift to hear and slow to speak. Bildad prophesied that the light of Job's tabernacle would be dark and that his candle would be put out. This was not true because, after the time of sufferings, Job's light shone and burned brighter than ever before.

2.   Zophar Accused Job of Being a Hypocrite and of Being Wicked (Job 20).

In his first conversation with Job, Zophar accused him of being a liar and a mocker. Then, in measuring Job's spiritual status by outward appearances and blessing, Zophar accused Job of being hypocritical and wicked. Zophar said, in so many words, that if Job were truly a child of God, then he would not be in his present condition. Sad to say, Zophar was exposing his ignorance of the Truth in God's Word, which the Apostle Peter later put into words: "Beloved, think it not strange concerning the fiery trial which is to try you, as though some strange thing happened unto you"(I Peter 4:12).

> And ye have forgotten the exhortation which speaketh unto you as unto children, My son, **despise not thou the chastening of the Lord,** nor faint when thou art rebuked of him: **For whom the Lord loveth he chasteneth, and scourgeth every son whom he receiveth.** If ye endure chastening, God dealeth with you as with sons; for what son is he whom the father chasteneth not? But if ye be without chastisement, whereof all are partakers, then are ye bastards, and not sons. Furthermore, we have had fathers of our flesh which corrected *us,* and we gave *them* reverence: shall we not much rather be in subjection unto the Father of spirits, and live? For they verily for a few days chastened *us* after their own pleasure; but he for *our* profit, that *we* might be partakers of his holiness. Now **no chastening for the present seemeth to be joyous, but grievous: nevertheless afterward it yieldeth the peaceable fruit of righteousness unto them which are exercised thereby** (Hebrews 12:5-11).

Zophar was not speaking from his knowledge of the Word of God, but out of the spirit of his own understanding and human reasoning. Zophar told Job that his blessings were gone because of his spiritual pride. How many times do we accuse others of the very thing of which we are guilty? We are always blind to our own faults.

3. Eliphaz Accused Job of Being a Hypocrite and of Being Wicked (Job 22).

Chapter twenty-two of the Book of Job relates another discourse by Eliphaz, wherein he not only reiterated the same accusations against Job but lengthened the list of Job's faults.

> *Is* **not thy wickedness great? and thine iniquities infinite?** For thou hast taken a pledge from thy brother for nought, and stripped the naked of their clothing. Thou hast not given water to the weary to drink, and thou hast withholden bread from the hungry. But *as for* the mighty man, he had the earth; and the honourable man dwelt in it. Thou hast sent widows away empty, and the arms of the fatherless have been broken. **Therefore snares** *are* **round about thee, and sudden fear troubleth thee;** (Job 22:5-10).

Eliphaz managed to heap more suffering upon Job by repeating and enlarging the same conclusions as Zophar. Eliphaz said, in essence, "Look at other wicked people and see what has happened to them. You are a hypocrite and wicked, so no wonder this suffering and these losses have come to you. You did not do what was right before God." Eliphaz and his companions condemned Job, in general, as a wicked man and a hypocrite, but none of them enumerated particulars. However, Eliphaz now positively and expressly charged Job with high crimes and misdemeanors. In one way, these friends were more guilty than the Sabeans and Chaldeans, for they tried to rob Job of his goodness and uprightness that God had given him. God had praised Job as the best man in the world, while his friends represented Job as the greatest villain in nature.

Innocence itself is no security against a false and foul tongue. Let us not think it strange when we are thus blackened. Let us learn to pass by evil reports and commit ourselves to Him Who judges righteously.

4.   Bildad Accused Job of Being Proud (Job 25).

Bildad exalted God and abased man. Bildad designed to possess Job with a reverence of God as though Job had none. He accused Job of being a proud man.

Job's double suffering is plain in these two Statures of Truth. Bildad returned, really, to persecute Job and add to his suffering instead of alleviating it. These friends had nothing of value to offer Job, as far as enlightening him concerning his present state of suffering. They were blind to God's Workings, yet God permitted it to be so that He could dig deeper into Job's heart, as Job made progress in spiritual growth in the Crucified Way.

Job's friends concluded that Job was a sinner, a hypocrite, a liar, a mocker, that he was wicked, that he winked at evil and wrong things in his life, that he was not right with God, according to outward evidence; thus, their list was endless. Bildad made the last thrust to push Job to the ground.

Next, in Job's responses, his friends' effect upon him came forth, and he began to "pour out" all his complaints. False accusations provoked the flesh and pride in Job, as they do in us.

C.   In His Suffering, Job Experienced Crucifixion of His Flesh.

God used his suffering, perpetrated by his friends, to show Job all his desires for pity, compassion, and the defense of his flesh.

Accusations will provoke one's pride to boast and brag in many ways. A Stature of Truth reveals Job's reaction to his friends' counsel.

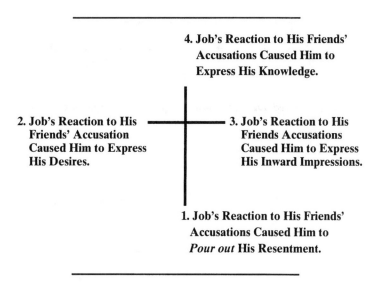

4. Job's Reaction to His Friends'
Accusations Caused Him to
Express His Knowledge.

2. Job's Reaction to His
Friends' Accusation
Caused Him to Express
His Desires.

3. Job's Reaction to His
Friends Accusations
Caused Him to Express
His Inward Impressions.

1. Job's Reaction to His Friends'
Accusations Caused Him to
Pour out His Resentment.

1.   Job's Reaction to His Friends' Accusations Caused Him to *Pour out* His Resentment.

The Fire of persecution eventually shows what is boiling inside of us, ready to burst forth and pour out. Things locked in our heart, which we have revealed to no one else, begin to pour out when we are under pressure. Along comes all our murmuring, complaining, and personal desires. Job's "pouring out" involved the following reactions:

(See stature of following page.)

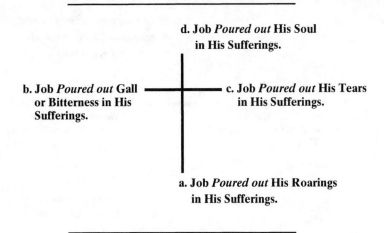

d. Job *Poured out* His Soul in His Sufferings.

b. Job *Poured out* Gall or Bitterness in His Sufferings.

c. Job *Poured out* His Tears in His Sufferings.

a. Job *Poured out* His Roarings in His Sufferings.

a. Job *Poured out* His Roarings in His Sufferings.

While Job sat on the ash heap, suffering in his body, he began to pour out his roarings. "For my sighing cometh before I eat, and *my roarings* are poured out like the waters" (Job 3:24).

Sorrow and suffering took away Job's appetite for his necessary food. His griefs and afflictions were his daily bread. So great was the extremity of his pain and anguish that he not only sighed but roared. His roarings were poured out like waters in a full and constant stream.

Actually, Job's accusations were against God, but he did not know it since he had no one to help him while the Fire was burning. Consequently, his roarings came out in such questions as these: "Why was I ever born? Why did the LORD not take me when I was first saved? For what do I have to live? Why has this happened to me?"

In his spiritual growth, Job's climb from despondency to delight carried him closer toward being an overcomer. His growth involved the following progressions:

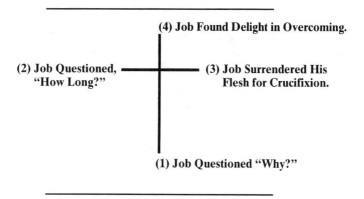

(4) Job Found Delight in Overcoming.

(2) Job Questioned,   **(3) Job Surrendered His**
    "How Long?"   **Flesh for Crucifixion.**

(1) Job Questioned "Why?"

(1)   Job Questioned "Why?"

***Why* died I not from the womb? *why* did I *not* give up
the ghost when I came out of the belly? *Why* did the
knees prevent me? or *why* the breasts that I should suck?**
(Job 3:11,12).

Why? Why? Why? Job poured out his roarings. The children of
Israel reacted in the same manner when they started their journey to
Canaan's Land, wishing themselves back in Egypt. "Why did you
bring us here? Do you intend to kill us in the wilderness?" they asked.

What is the reason we ask "Why?" It is simply because we are
blind to and ignorant of God's Purpose and doings. Why can I not do
what I want, *when* and *where* I want, instead of *your* way, God?
Romans 8:28, answers the *why* to everything: "And we know that a*ll*
things work together for good to them that love God, to them who are
the called according to his purpose." Sometimes, we mentally
acknowledge the Truth of this verse, but when we finally learn this
Truth in our hearts, we will no longer need to ask "Why?" Romans
8:28 gives God's Purpose for *all things,* whether pleasurable or painful
for us, which is to be be conformed to the *image* of His Son.

(2)   Job Questioned "How Long?"

After we have learned the answer to *why,* we cry, "LORD, *how long* will this circumstance continue? How long am I going to have to put up with this pain? How long is this Fire going to burn, LORD?"

The reason we ask *"How long?"* is due to our lack of long-suffering, as well as the rebellion in our flesh and in our *self.* We want God to cut off our suffering, but only God knows how long it will take for us to surrender our will to His Headship so that some portion of our *old man* or old heart can be conformed to His Image.

(3)   Job Surrendered His Flesh for Crucifixion.

We must be willing to stay in the Fire or any adverse circumstance for as long as God deems necessary, for we do not know our hearts — only God does. In fact, if we are wise, we will want to stay for the length of God's time and learn our lesson so that we will not have to repeat it. We need to stay in God's "little red school house" until we "graduate."

(4)   Job Found Delight in Overcoming.

The culmination of surrender is delight — delight in the Fire of suffering until our own wills are surrendered to God's Will. This delight is gained only as we become acquainted with Christ's Humility. This delight comes as we begin to find the treasures of His Humility in our sufferings.

We must prostrate ourselves to God's Will until we find the thrill of the *Fan of His Humility* — the class of Humility that separates us from the chaff of our own wills. We must bow to God's Will until we find the thrill of the *Harp of His Humility* — the class of Humility that plays a melody in our hearts because God is having His Way. We must stay under God's Headship until we experience the thrill of the *Shaft of His Humility* — the class of Humility that supports us with the strength to suffer so that God's Will may be accomplished in our hearts and lives; then, we will find His Delight — the Delight the Son had in doing His Father's Will and the Delight the Father had in His Son.

b. Job *Poured out* Gall or Bitterness in His Sufferings.

> His archers compass me round about, he cleaveth my
> reins asunder, and doth not spare; **he poureth out my**
> **gall upon the ground** (Job 16:13).

Gall speaks of bitterness. Gall is earthly and cannot be offered to God, for it is of the flesh. When there is bitterness in our hearts toward someone, it will pour out of our mouths, for out of the abundance of the heart the mouth speaketh.

The carnal heart has an amazing capacity for bitterness, which shows up when someone puts us in the Fire of suffering; whether at home, at church, or on the job, our bitterness will come out. Suffering results in retaliation and will start a Fire in the person who has made us suffer because misery loves company.

> Looking diligently lest any man fail of the grace of
> God; **lest any root of bitterness springing up trouble**
> ***you*, and thereby many be defiled** (Hebrews 12:15).

Paul explained that, if our eyes are not open to see what God is doing, we will pour out gall, and it will touch and affect others. Bitterness will defile others as well as ourselves. It will pour out Fire that we do not know we are capable of producing.

God wants our hearts emptied of the works of the flesh. The great octopus of *self* has two main legs: one is the leg of hatred that breeds bitterness and gall, and one is the leg of love for natural or worldly things that fill us with bitterness when we do not get what we want. These two legs must be cut off if we want to go on with the LORD Jesus Christ and glow in His Spiritual Stature until we are conformed to His Image.

c.   Job Poured out His Tears in His Sufferings.

My friends scorn me: *but* **mine eye poureth out** *tears*
unto God (Job 16:20).

As Job was reaching out for human sympathy, human pity, and
human understanding, but receiving none from his friends, it caused
him to "pour out" tears of brokenness to God.

God dwells with those of a broken and contrite heart. We should
never despise our tears, for God has a tear bottle wherein He bottles
up our tears — not fleshly tears of self-pity — but spiritual tears that
are poured out to God. Tears of intercession and travail accompany
our going on for God, and these tears are precious to Him. Tears,
when sanctified to God, give ease to troubled spirits. It is a great comfort to know that God regards the tears that are poured out to Him.

d.   Job Poured out His Soul in His Sufferings.

And now **my soul is poured out** upon me; the days of
affliction have taken hold upon me (Job 30:16).

The terror and trouble that seized Job's soul were the sorest part
of his calamity. If he looked forward, he saw no hope; he just saw
everything frightful and dreadful. If he endeavored to shake off his
terrors, they returned furiously upon him. If he tried to escape from
them, they pursued his soul as swiftly and violently as the wind. If
he looked back, he saw all the good he had formerly enjoyed that
had been removed from him. If he looked within, he found his soul
unable to bear his infirmity; therefore, it was poured out upon him.
His soul was like water spilled upon the ground.

After his tears, Job's soul was broken and melted, and all the
pride and bigotry of his soul and mind were poured out.

God loves a poured-out soul. God knows and hears what is in
our hearts and minds; still, He delights to have us pour it out to Him

in our own language, as we express freely what is in our hearts. God hears and answers prayer, and God will come soon to assist us in our weaknesses.

Job had to endure much suffering to learn to "pour out" his soul. There is a way that we can "pour out" our soul through suffering that is not possible at any other time, even though the Spirit makes intercession through us. When we realize the price that Job had to pay, then we realize how valuable spiritual treasures are in God's sight.

2.   Job's Reaction to His Friends' Accusations Caused Him to Express His Desires.

A desire for deeper spiritual experiences is formed in us only as we permit it to be.

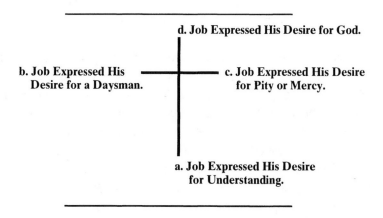

d. Job Expressed His Desire for God.

b. Job Expressed His Desire for a Daysman.

c. Job Expressed His Desire for Pity or Mercy.

a. Job Expressed His Desire for Understanding.

a. Job Expressed His Desire for Understanding.

Teach me, and I will hold my tongue: and **cause me to understand wherein I have erred** (Job 6:24).

It is the true character of every *honest* man to want his mistakes rectified and to be made to understand wherein he has erred.

As a result of all his suffering, Job desired understanding, which can come only from the LORD. His friends could not give Job understanding; in fact, they did not teach him anything, for he knew more than they did. Job wanted to understand wherein he had erred. His friends did not have the knowledge to help; they only confused Job.

It is great to understand where we have erred so that we may acknowledge right words, though they be contrary to our former sentiments. When understanding comes, right words are both forcible and acceptable.

b.   Job Expressed His Desire for a Daysman.

Neither is there any daysman betwixt us, *that* might lay his hand upon us both (Job 9:33).

Job acknowledged that God is not a man, as Job was; therefore, God's Thoughts and Ways were infinitely above his. Man cannot measure God by his creatures. Man is foolish and weak, frail and fickle, but God is Omniscient, Omnipotent, and without even a shadow of turning; He has no variableness. Man is a dependent, dying creature, but God is the Independent, Immortal Creator — the Originator and Sustainer of all life. Job needed a Daysman, a Mediator, an Arbitrator, or an Umpire to adjust the differences between himself and God.

Since Job desired a Daysman or a Mediator, he actually desired Jesus. Jesus Christ is the blessed "Daysman" Who mediates between Heaven and Earth and Who has taken hold of God the Father, on one hand, and has taken hold of miserable, mortal man on the other hand.

In the Fire of suffering, we often desire comfort from others more than Jesus' comfort. We need to run to our prayer closet and get alone with Jesus and let Him put us in contact with God.

Blessings and prosperity show up in our self-life so that we have a tendency to esteem ourselves better than others. We desire possession and position more than we desire the Daysman to put us in contact with God. Sometimes, God must separate us from outward prosperity and friends for the purpose of bringing us closer to Him.

c.   Job Expressed His Desire for Pity or Mercy.

Have pity upon me, have pity upon me, O ye my friends;
for the hand of God hath touched me (Job 19:21).

Job desired pity or compassion. Sometimes, with riches, one gets independent and feels that he has need of nothing. When God puts us down, the need for pity or compassion arises until He has us in our right place.

Job knew that God's Hand was on him and that he was not his own, but Job did not know *why*. He begged his friends for pity and mercy in the most moving, melting language, but he never received any. Surely, when God's Hand is upon us to lead us into greater places with Him, the least others can do is to show us pity and compassion.

d.   Job Expressed His Desire for God.

Oh that I knew where I might find him! *that* **I might come** *even* **to his seat!** I would order *my* cause before him, and fill my mouth with arguments (Job 23:3,4).

Because of all his intense suffering, Job's desire was for God Himself and His Throne so that he could to make known his condition and requests. Fire purifies even our desires.

A reward, prize, or payoff gives birth to desire. When our income and spending are done without regard to our LORD, sometimes God must remove our paycheck in order to get our desire in the right place.

3.   Job's Reaction to His Friends' Accusations Caused Him to Express His Inward Impressions.

Frequently, the impressions we get are wrong. God is the only One Who knows and sees rightly. Our minds are too cluttered with wrong, sinful impressions to have fair, honest judgment since we cannot see inside our hearts. God permits impressions to show us what is inside us. We surmise somebody is against us, but usually this is not true. Exaggerations often give false impressions.

What do we do when we have an impression that someone has done something against us? Do we follow the scriptural pattern and go to our brother or sister and seek to correct and to clarify our impression, or do we talk behind their backs, letting a sour spirit rise up toward them and, consequently, be too proud to acknowledge that we could be wrong in our impression? Possibly our silence leaves a question mark or a bad taste, and this is the most dangerous of all because it leaves room for so much imagination.

The Serpent in the Garden of Eden used the questioning approach when he asked Adam-female, "Hath God said?" Doubt stirs the imagination through meditation. This can develop into a very ugly ordeal if we pass on these impressions to others.

a. Job Felt His Friends Considered Him to Be Inferior to Them.

> **But I have understanding as well as you; I *am* not inferior to you:** yea, who knoweth not such things as these? I am *as* one mocked of his neighbour, who calleth upon God, and he answereth him: the just upright *man is* laughed to scorn (Job 12:3,4).

God allows impressions to test how much love we have. Love covers a multitude of sins. Until we have grown in spiritual stature, our tendency is to cover our own sins, while we expose others' sins. God tries us to see if we will cover up for our brother or tell it abroad. It is a great mystery how we clearly see our brother's fleshly self-life, yet we can love him sufficiently to cover up and make excuses for him until God brings him to the place of crucifixion in the matter.

> No doubt but ye *are* the people, and **wisdom shall die with you** (Job 12:2).

What ye know, *the same* do I know also: **I *am* not infe-rior unto you** (Job 13:2).

God let Job get the impression that his friends thought him infe-rior. Unless our flesh is crucified, we will do just what Job did; we will say, "I know more than you do. I am not inferior!" In the end, Job's impression caused him to humble himself even more. If these friends had never made him feel inferior, he would not have had to humble himself before them.

b. Job Felt His Friends Were Miserable Comforters.

I have heard many such things: **miserable comforters *are* ye all** (Job 16:2).

Another impression Job had of his friends was that they were miserable comforters. Again, Job had to be humbled in order to return to his friends and do good to them.

4. Job's Reaction to His Friends' Accusations Caused Him to Express His Knowledge.

More of Job's flesh came to the foreground as God allowed him to be put through the Fire of suffering so that he might see the purifi-cation of his *self* that he so sorely needed. This is not only true for Job, but for all who press on in the Crucified Way.

Some of the lessons Job learned are recorded in chapter twenty-one. First of all, the prosperity of the wicked refuted the view that Job had been punished because of secret sin. In so many words, Job could say, "Go ahead and mock me; laugh about it, my friends, if you think I am receiving punishment as a hypocrite, a secret sinner. Look at the wicked; they live and do not seem to have any problems. The wicked are in power throughout the world. How do you explain their prosperity? Look at the wicked; they are blessed by having their children before them. Thieves and robbers have not had their possessions stolen, but I have," said Job. In other words, the wicked rejected God, lived to old age, had an easy life, lived in wealth, yet, here was Job, a servant of the LORD, and he was sick, afflicted, and suffering. How could this be reconciled? Thus, Job gained the knowledge that prosperity is not a sign of God's blessing, nor is it God's expressed pleasure over an individual's life.

In chapter nineteen, Job's flesh poured out more roarings, and the reason God had to put Job in the Fire of suffering becomes more clear. Job's *self*-life is pictured as he "poured out."

It is amazing how few people know what the Book of Job is all about. Notice the "me," the "I," and the "my," of *self* that poured out of Job in chapter nineteen.

(See chart on following page.)

Verse	"MY"	"ME"	"I"
2	*my* soul	break *me*	
4			*I* have erred
5	*my* reproach	against *me* plead against *me* overthrown *me* compassed *me*	
7			*I* cry *I* am not heard *I* cry aloud
8	*my* way *my* paths		*I* cannot pass
9	*my* glory *my* head	stripped *me*	
10		destroyed *me*	*I* am gone
11		against *me* counteth *me*	
12	*my* tabernacle	against *me*	
13	*my* brethren	far from *me* estranged from *me*	
14	*my* kinsfolk *my* familiar friends	forgotten *me*	
15	*my* maids	count *me*	*I* am an alien
16	*my* mouth	gave *me* no answer	*I* called my servant *I* entreated him
17	*my* breath *my* wife		*I* entreated
18		despised *me* spoke against *me*	
19	*my* inward friends	abhorred *me* against *me*	*I* love
20	*my* bone *my* skin *my* flesh *my* teeth		*I* am escaped
21	*my* friends	upon *me* touched *me*	
22	*my* flesh	persecute *me*	
23	*my* words		
25	*my* redeemer		*I* know
26	*my* skin *my* flesh		*I* see God
27	*my* reins	consumed with *me*	*I* shall see
28		found in *me*	
Totals	"MY" 26 times	"ME" 24 times	"I" 15 times (65)

55

Job's *self,* flesh, and spiritual pride manifested themselves in the midst of the Fire of suffering. God put Job in the Fire to strip him of all his *self*-glory.

Notice also, the "me," the "I," and the "my' of *self* that poured out of Job in chapter twenty-nine. It sounds comparable to chapter nineteen.

(See chart on following page.)

Verse	"MY"	"ME"	"I"
2		God preserved *me*	*I* were as in months past
3	*my* head		*I* walked through darkness
4	*my* youth *my* tabernacle		*I* was in the days
5	*my* children	Almighty was yet with *me* were about *me*	
6.		rock poured *me*	*I* washed my steps with butter
7	*my* seat		*I* went out to the gate *I* prepared
8 11		young men saw *me* ear heard *me* it blessed *me* eye saw *me* gave witness to *me*	
13		came upon *me*	*I* delivered the poor *I* caused the widow's heart to sing
14 15	*my* judgment	it clothed *me*	*I* put on righteousness *I* was blind feet was *I* to the lame *I* was a father to the poor *I* knew not *I* searched out
17			*I* searched out *I* brake the jaws
18	*my* nest *my* days		*I* said *I* shall die *I* shall multiply
19 20	*my* root *my* glory *my* bow *my* hand	flesh in *me*	
21 22	*my* counsel *my* words *my* speech	unto *me*	
23 24 25	*my* countenance	waited for *me*	*I* laughed on them *I* chose out their way
Totals	"MY" 16 times	"ME" 14 times	"I" 20 times (50)

Job, chapter 19 — 65

Job, chapter 29 — <u>50</u>

150 Total Times

While Job knew more about God's Power-side than His Nature-side, he wished himself back where he was before God started working on his flesh. It takes Christ's Crucified-side, the furnace of affliction, to have His Nature worked in us. Crucifixion implies suffering and death, and only when our flesh has died can God impart His Divine Nature unto us. Judging from all the personal pronouncements of Job's "I's," "me's," and "my's," it looked as though Job accomplished everything by himself and that God was nowhere around.

In Job 29:18, he boasted of tomorrow, which God's Word clearly commands us *not* to do. Verse twenty-two shows that Job had been the spokesman, and there was no talking back to him. Job's pride had to be reduced to the place of humility. This was the only route that God could take Job; thus, He permitted these situations to bring Job low in spirit so that, in due time, He could exalt Job.

The foregoing Stature of Truth in this chapter has revealed Job's reaction to all his suffering. First, Job's suffering caused him to "pour out" in roaring, in gall or bitterness, and in tears, as he "poured out" his soul. Second, his suffering honed his desires for understanding, for a daysman, for pity, and for God. Third, the suffering inflicted by Job's friends caused him to receive impressions and to speak from his knowledge.

(By now, the Book of Job should to be speaking to each of us, causing us to evaluate ourselves in God's sight in a new way.)

Job eventually moved to the Resurrection-side of God's Scales in his time of suffering and in his experiences with God.

D.   In His Suffering, Job Experienced Resurrection Power.

(See stature on following page.)

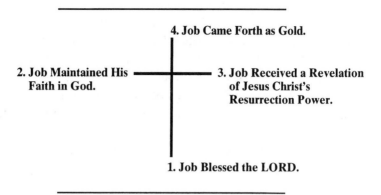

4. Job Came Forth as Gold.

2. Job Maintained His Faith in God. —— 3. Job Received a Revelation of Jesus Christ's Resurrection Power.

1. Job Blessed the LORD.

1. Job Blessed the LORD.

Then Job arose, and rent his mantle, and shaved his head, and fell down upon the ground, and worshipped, And said, Naked came I out of my mother's womb, and naked shall I return thither: **the LORD gave, and the LORD hath taken away; blessed be the name of the LORD** (Job 1:20,21).

When Job was stripped of his children and his possessions, he stood the test. His response was, "Blessed be the LORD." His actions proved Satan a liar, for Satan had said that if God allowed him to put Job under affliction that Job would curse God. Instead, Job acknowledged God's Hand in the situation, both in the mercies he formerly had enjoyed and in the afflictions he then suffered.

2. Job Maintained His Faith in God.

Though he slay me, yet will I trust in him: but I will maintain mine own ways before him (Job 13:15).

Job still maintained faith in his heart, even though he suffered in his mind and in his body. Job's friends also caused him much mental anguish. Job concluded that, even though the LORD slay him, he still would trust Him. We all should desire to attain this high expression of faith. To trust God's Nature when He seems to come forth against us as an enemy is to ascend to the highest hill of faith. Job said that he would not turn his back on God and curse Him and die, as his wife suggested. Even in death, Job vowed he would trust God. Having a living faith that will trust in the midst of affliction is a great thing.

3.   Job Received a Revelation of Jesus Christ's Resurrection Power.

To our knowledge, there was no Written Word in Job's day; yet, by faith, he had the revelation to believe in the Second Coming of Christ and the resurrection of the body. Job was surrendered, even to die. "Though after my skin worms destroy this body, yet in my flesh shall I see God," so testified Job.

> For **I know** *that* **my redeemer liveth, and** *that* **he shall stand at the latter** *day* **upon the earth: And** *though* **after my skin** *worms* **destroy this** *body***, yet in my flesh shall I see God:** (Job 19:25,26)

Job's knowledge of death, destruction, and dissolution of his body in the grave did not discourage his hope of the resurrection. The glorious Truth of the resurrection of the body burned and shone brightly in Job's heart.

4.   Job Came Forth as Gold.

> But he knoweth the way that I take: *when* **he hath tried me, I shall come forth as gold** (Job 23:10).

Job contented himself with the thought that God knew the way that he had taken. Although Job did not understand what God was doing, he still chose God's Way. Job was comforted that it was only a trial. A trial is not intended for hurt, but for honour and benefit, and when one is sufficiently tried, he shall come forth out of the furnace of affliction and not be left to be consumed in it as dross or reprobate silver. Job was thrilled with the anticipation of being brought forth as gold, pure and precious to his Refiner, even God. He would come forth as approved and improved gold. Therefore, Job's furnace of affliction proved to be a blessing in disguise. Job was growing in spiritual stature with each experience of suffering. By faith, he saw the purpose and reward of his trials.

This knowledge will also give us courage to press on in the Fire of persecution and suffering since we know that we will come forth as *pure gold,* just as Job did.

Job's sufferings thus far have laid the foundation for his experience with Elihu or with God and for greater spiritual fruitfulness in his spiritual life.

There is a Glory that comes with a deeper revelation of ourselves and of God that we attain through suffering.

> For I reckon that **the sufferings of this present time *are* not worthy *to be compared* with the glory which shall be revealed in us** (Romans 8:18).

May we ever keep our eyes on Eternity and the Prize at the end of our way.

Chapter Three

Job's Experience With Elihu

This chapter presents the second major Stature of Truth in our study of the Book of Job and relates Job's experience with Elihu. Elihu was a type of the LORD Jesus Christ as a Daysman and a Mediator. Elihu's name signifies "my God is he."

Elihu acted as an agent between Job and God; he was a "go-between." Usually, young men are the disputants and old men the mediators, but, in Job's case, the old men were the disputants, and a young man by the name of Elihu was raised up to be the mediator.

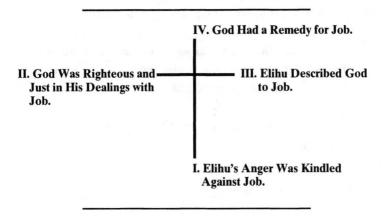

IV. God Had a Remedy for Job.

II. God Was Righteous and Just in His Dealings with Job.

III. Elihu Described God to Job.

I. Elihu's Anger Was Kindled Against Job.

I.   Elihu's Anger Was Kindled Against Job.

Then was kindled the wrath of Elihu the son of Barachel the Buzite, of the kindred of Ram: **against Job was his wrath kindled,** because he justified himself rather than God. **Also against his three friends was his wrath kindled,**

because they had found no answer, and *yet* had condemned Job (Job 32:2,3).

Up to this point, Elihu had kept silent since he was a younger man
and had respect for older, aged men. Listening in silence to their dis-
courses, Elihu discerned, by the Spirit of God, that these friends were
not a source of help to Job. God began to give true understanding to
Elihu, as shown in Job 32:4-17. Elihu was bursting to give the Word
from God to Job and to give him the answer to his problem of suffering.

Elihu began to speak because he was angry. When he had made
his observations upon the dispute, he did not go away and malign
the disputants by striking them secretly with a malicious, censorious
tongue, but what he had to say, he said to their faces so that they
might vindicate themselves if they could.

The fleshly spirit in both Job and his three friends had caused
Elihu's anger. In any human dispute there is flesh or *self* on both
sides, and a mediator must recognize this regardless of whom it comes
through, thereby showing no respect of persons.

Elihu was angry at Job because he did not speak as reverently of
God as he should have. He took more care and pains to clear himself
from the imputation of unrighteousness in his affliction than he made
to clear God of unrighteousness in the affliction. Job was more concerned for his own honour than for God's honour. He should have justified God and cleared His Glory, first, then left his reputation in
God's Hands. A gracious, surrendered heart is jealous for God's Glory
and Honour. We do not breach the laws of meekness and humility if
we are angry with our friends when they are offensive to God.

On the other hand, Elihu was angry at Job's friends because
they had not conducted themselves as charitably toward Job as they
should have. They had judged him to be a hypocrite and a wicked
man, yet they could not prove him so, nor could they disprove the
evidences he produced of his integrity. Elihu was displeased with
their mistakes and mismanagement concerning Job's affliction.

His three friends had condemned Job without an answer, for
they were not spiritual enough to discern the Truth. It is a serious

matter to condemn someone without being able to show them a way to overcome the weaknesses of their *self*-life. When Elihu realized that no answer was forthcoming from the three men, his wrath was kindled. Naturally, older people should know more about the LORD, but that is not always the case. Great men are not always wise, neither do the aged always understand judgment.

II.   God Was Righteous and Just in His Dealings with Job.

Chapter thirty-three of the Book of Job relates the second thing Job experienced with Elihu. With his heart bursting to overflowing, Elihu began to expound to Job the revelation of God's dealings with him.

Elihu was a picture of Jesus Christ, the Daysman or Mediator for whom Job had prayed. God is faithful to hear and to answer our prayers that prove our sincerity and desire to grow in Jesus' Spiritual Stature, so He will send someone to lead us, or He will come Himself, if necessary, to answer our need.

> Behold, **I *am* according to thy wish in God's stead:** I
> also am formed out of the clay (Job 33:6).

Job had pathetically wished for a Daysman, a Mediator, to plead his cause with God when he said, "O, that one might plead for a man with God" (Job 16:21). So Elihu undertook to plead God's cause with Job and to show Job wherein he had affronted God and what complaints God had against him. Elihu let Job know that his appeals or complaints to God should have been made through him as a mediator. Elihu promised that his discourse would not make Job afraid, nor would his hand be heavy upon him.

If we are to succeed in rightly convincing men of God's Justice and Care, it must be by reason, not by rumor, and be by fair arguing, not by a heavy hand.

Also, Elihu was a picture of Jesus Christ, the Saviour, Who was formed out of clay. Elihu, the wanted daysman, the wanted mediator, came to fulfill Job's wishes and to stand in the Mediator's place by taking hold of Job with one hand and taking hold of God with the other hand.

Jesus Christ is ever mindful of His own, acting as a Mediator by taking hold of us with one of His Hands and taking hold of God with His other Hand.

Elihu reminded Job, in verses twelve and thirteen, that Job was not quite as clean and innocent as he thought. God wanted to reveal more to Job of his *self*-life. Elihu declared that Job was not just in proclaiming complete innocence and cleanliness.

There was a difference between the charge Elihu exhibited against Job and that which was preferred against him by his other friends. They would not admit that Job was just at all; Elihu, alone, said, "In *this*, in saying *this*, thou art not just." In other words, Elihu told Job that he was not dealing justly with God. To be just is to render to all people their dues. We do not render to God His due, nor are we just to Him if we fail to acknowledge His Equity and Kindness in all the dispensations of His Providence toward us: that He is righteous in all His Ways and that, however it be, GOD IS GOOD! Job had spoken admirably well concerning God's Greatness, His irresistible Power, His incontestable Sovereignty, His terrible Majesty, and His unsearchable Immensity, but he had not spoken well of the Holiness and Righteousness of God's Will in the affliction he suffered.

Elihu reminded Job that God is greater than man; therefore, this Truth should have silenced all Job's ill-natured, ill-favored reflections and complaints against God's Will that had brought suffering to his life.

Since God has all Wisdom and all Power, it is absurd and unreasonable to find fault with Him, seeing He is Righteous and Holy. It is foolish to strive against God. Those who complain about God are striving against Him, impeaching Him, bringing an action against Him. It is irrational for us foolish, weak, sinful creations to strive with the Infinite God, Who is under no obligation to give reasons for His Purposes and Designs in our lives. He is not bound either to justify His own proceedings nor to satisfy our demands or inquiries; His Judgments justify themselves.

A. Elihu Told how God Deals with Man in Dreams and Visions.

Elihu, by revelation from God, told Job how God deals with men. In Job, chapter thirty-three, Elihu mentions God's ways of dealing: through dreams, visions, and afflictions.

> **For God speaketh once, yea twice,** *yet man* **perceiveth it not. In a dream, in a vision of the night,** when deep sleep falleth upon men, in slumberings upon the bed; (Job 33:14,15).

Job complained that God had kept him in the dark concerning the reasons for His dealings with him; therefore, Job concluded that God had dealt with him as an enemy. But Elihu revealed to Job that, although God had spoken, Job had not perceived, nor had he taken heed, regarded, discerned, nor understood what God was trying to tell him. Unaware of God's Voice, Job had not received the things revealed to him. They were foolishness to him, so he had stopped his ear; he had stood in his own light; and he had rejected God's Counsel against him; thus, he was none the wiser.

Elihu showed how God teaches and admonishes the children of men by their own consciences. The proper season and opportunity for His admonitions are in the nighttime, when men are asleep upon their beds. Then, they are in a state of relaxation, having retired from the world and its business and conversations, and can dream and have visions. This is a good time for men to retire into their own hearts and let God commune with them while they are solitary and still. For example, God spoke to Abimelech by night in a dream concerning Abraham's wife:

> But **God came to Abimelech in a dream by night,** and said to him, Behold, thou *art but* a dead man, for **the woman which thou hast taken;** for she **is a man's wife** (Genesis 20:3).

Also, God warned Laban in a dream not to mistreat Jacob.

> And **God came to Laban** the Syrian **in a dream** by
> night, and said unto him, Take heed that thou speak
> not to Jacob either good or bad (Genesis 31:24).

God confirmed this manner of His speaking when He told Moses,
Aaron, and Miriam that He would speak to His Prophet in a dream.

> And he said, **Hear now my words: If there be a
> prophet among you, *I* the LORD will make myself
> known unto him in a vision, *and* will speak unto him in
> a dream** (Numbers 12:6).

God warned Joseph in a dream concerning Jesus' conception,
and, again, after Jesus' birth, God warned Joseph about Herod's
intent to kill Jesus.

> But while he thought on these things, behold, **the
> angel of the Lord appeared unto him in a dream,** say-
> ing, Joseph, thou son of David, fear not to take unto
> thee Mary thy wife: for that which is conceived in her
> is of the Holy Ghost (Matthew 1:20).

> And when they were departed, behold, the angel of the
> **Lord appeareth to Joseph in a dream,** saying, Arise, and
> take the young child and his mother, and flee into Egypt,
> and be thou there until I bring thee word: for Herod will
> seek the young child to destroy him (Matthew 2:13).

In the same way, by dreams and visions, God made known to
Pharaoh and to Nebuchadnezzar the things that should come to
pass "hereafter."

Conscience is God's deputy that works even in the night season
to convict and reproach man for things that are displeasing to God.

He opens the ear by taking away that which stops the ear so that conviction finds or forces its way into the heart; thus, He makes souls to receive the deep and lasting impressions of His Mind and His Will. The Design and Purpose of these Works of God is to pluck sin, and particularly pride, from man's heart.

Sometimes, we blame the Devil for our dreams when it is God dealing with us in order to show us ourselves. Psychologists interpret dreams as a person's subconscious thoughts being personified, as they take on various forms and become occupied in sundry activities. In fact, thoughts are withheld and stored in our subconscious minds, especially things we want repressed, and we do not realize they are there. God deals with us to cleanse and rid our minds of such thoughts, but we fail to recognize what He is doing.

For example, we may dream about someone hitting someone else. This is nothing but a thought of rebellion, hatred, or retaliation hidden in our subconscious mind. Perhaps someone has felt repulsion or resentment toward another individual; then, he has pushed the matter down into his subconscious mind. Later, at night in a dream, this feeling and thought stands up, personified, and begins to war and fight with someone. Or we may dream of being very successful, such as directing a huge crowd, teaching many people, preaching to multitudes. This is superiority pride manifesting itself. Or we may dream quite the opposite, such as finding ourselves down in a low place, on the bottom of the pile, struggling to get up. This is inferiority pride manifesting itself. Through our dreams, God speaks, reveals and exposes what is really down in our hearts. Would to God that we would hear, listen, understand, and respond to His revelations of our inner self.

Thus, dreams and visions are two ways God speaks to try to show us our fleshly attitudes and dispositions before He resorts to affliction, which is the third way He deals with mankind. Apparently God had spoken in dreams and visions to show Job his spiritual pride, but he had refused to see it.

He is chastened also with pain upon his bed, and the multitude of his bones with strong *pain*: (Job 33:19).

Job's life shows how God deals through afflictions. Job finally began to learn and to open his eyes to the Truth of God's dealings. He began to understand what his afflictions were all about. Job had complained much about his affliction and had judged that God was angry with him, just as his friends had judged. But Elihu, the mediator, showed Job that they all were mistaken, for God, in His Mercy and Love, often afflicts our bodies with gracious Designs for good for our souls so that our souls might grow in compassion and long-suffering.

The pain in Job's body that racked his very bones, was strong and acute. It was inwardly rooted pain, not in one bone, but in the multitude of his bones. What frail and vile bodies we have!

Although we walk in obedience and in the directive Will of God, there are times in which we go through the same suffering and affliction, to the end that our souls might be transformed into the Likeness and Image of Jesus Christ. The Bible speaks of our afflicting ourselves, which is what we do when we fast. The body may suffer much pain with continual loss of sleep during a prolonged fast. Such a fast is profitable, for God then puts our fleshly man to death and crucifies our pride in order that the Spiritual Man might increase in Wisdom, Understanding, and Knowledge in the things of God.

God's using afflictions to minister spiritual benefits was a great revelation to Job. His other three friends were unable to do this, but Elihu revealed these spiritual lessons to Job. The others could not conceive that suffering was part of the road to spiritual maturity. What a blessing we experience when this Truth is revealed to us, and we believe it!

B.   God Has a Reason for Giving Dreams and Visions.

Then he openeth the ears of men, and sealeth their instruction, (Job 33:16).

This verse uncovers God's Reason for giving us dreams and visions, which is to open our ears. The word *open* means to uncover, reveal, denude. God uses dreams and visions to *seal* or to *make an end* of men's instructions. God tries to speak to us and show us what is wrong with us so that we will humble ourselves and lay aside our wrongs; hence, we can enter into a deeper and higher walk with Him.

There is a Stature of Truth embedded in Job 33:17, 18, which gives God's Reason or Purpose for dreams and visions.

That he may withdraw man *from his* purpose, and hide pride from man. He keepeth back his soul from the pit, and his life from perishing by the sword (Job 33:17,18).

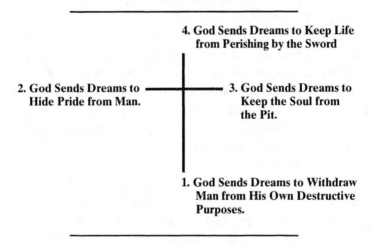

1. God Sends Dreams to Withdraw Man from His Own Destructive Purposes.

God wants to withdraw us from our fleshly desires and our own selfish way. He seeks to change the temper of our minds and the course of our lives, to change our evil dispositions and stubborn inclinations, and to prevent us from falling into some particular sin so that He may cause us to leave off the world and the flesh, thus helping us to walk God's Walk.

2.   God Sends Dreams to Hide Pride from Man.

God's Purpose in sending dreams is to bring to our knowledge our need for Jesus Christ's Humility so that we might be patterned after it. Pride makes people eager and resolute in the prosecution of their own purposes; therefore, God withdraws men from their purposes by mortifying their pride.

3.   God Sends Dreams to Keep the Soul from the Pit.

God has prepared a place for the proud and haughty, but in Mercy and Love, God sends dreams and visions to man to admonish his conscience so that he will withdraw from his sinful way and thereby keep his soul from the Pit.

4.   God Sends Dreams to Keep Life from Perishing by the Sword.

God, through dreams and visions, hopes to deter the human soul from rushing onto the sword of destruction. Thus, He *saves* them from perishing by the Sword of Divine Vengeance so that iniquity will not be their ruin. We, on the other hand, *need* the Sword of the Word of God in our Christian walk in order for It to cut and sever us from the many things in our lives that are unlike Jesus Christ.

III.   Elihu Described God to Job.

The third thing Job experienced in his encounter with Elihu was having Elihu tell him what God was like. The three friends tried to describe God, but they knew less than Job did, so what they said was of little spiritual value to Job. To see God is to see ourselves and our own needs. Job knew considerable about the LORD, but there was much he did not know. It takes a vision of God to solve our problems.

First, Elihu told Job of God's Purity and why He is Pure. Then, he told Job about God's Praise, His Power, and His Possessions.

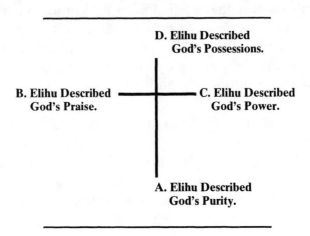

D. Elihu Described
God's Possessions.

B. Elihu Described
God's Praise.

C. Elihu Described
God's Power.

A. Elihu Described
God's Purity.

A.   Elihu Described God's Purity.

Elihu came to minister to Job about God's Purity. Job knew that God is Pure, yet it had never been quickened to his heart, or he would not have complained. Beloved, we are just as guilty as Job. If we really knew God's Purity in our hearts, rather than only in our minds, our murmuring and complaining in affliction and suffering would cease.

When we complain, we are saying, "God, You are unjust. You are unfair. You are not pure. You are unrighteous." Our words of complaint say, "I cannot depend on You nor trust You to meet my needs." What an awful, horrifying accusation! How precious it is for us to grow in our Christian experience to the place that, regardless of the Fire of suffering we are enduring, we can say, "LORD, You are too pure to allow this circumstance without having a good Reason or Purpose for it. All things work together for our good. All of God's Ways and Dealings are pure; therefore, we need to admit and recognize this to be true.

God's Purity is manifested in the following ways:

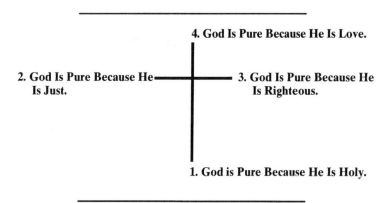

4. God Is Pure Because He Is Love.

2. God Is Pure Because He Is Just.

3. God Is Pure Because He Is Righteous.

1. God is Pure Because He Is Holy.

1. God Is Pure Because He Is Holy.

Therefore hearken unto me ye men of understanding: **far be it from God,** *that he should do* **wickedness; and** *from* **the Almighty,** *that he should commit* **iniquity** (Job 34:10).

Elihu elaborated on God's Purity and revealed it to Job. God is Pure because He is Holy. There is no wickedness nor impurity in God. Had God afflicted Job for nought, He would not have been pure. If God had let Satan bring affliction on Job without a purpose, He would have been a wicked God. Until one recognizes that God is Holy, it is impossible to have complete confidence in Him; instead, we will murmur and complain about our circumstances.

God cannot do wickedness nor can the Almighty commit iniquity. Wickedness and iniquity are inconsistent with the Perfection of God's Nature and the Purity of His Will. God neither can nor will He do a wrong thing nor will He deal unkindly with any man.

Because God is infinitely Perfect and Holy, He cannot permit needless afflictions and sufferings. What a wonderful revelation of His Holy Nature! We must humble ourselves in all afflicting circumstances and look for the good and not accuse God by murmuring and complaining.

2. God Is Pure Because He Is Just.

Yea, surely **God will not do wickedly, neither will the Almighty pervert judgment** (Job 34:12).

Elihu continued teaching Job about God's Purity by letting Job know that God is Just. He is Pure because He is Holy, and He is Pure because He is Just. Since God is Almighty, nothing else can be true other than that He is Just. God will not pervert Judgment on anyone. God's Purity reveals His Holiness and His Justice. Although he is Almighty, He never uses His Power to support injustice. God's distributive Justice makes Him give to every man according to his works.

Job's affliction had fallen on him because he needed it for his own good. God is not a respecter of persons, and He is too Pure to bring anything across our pathway that is not necessary for us as a Christian. God has a Purpose for us, and He knows the way to take us higher; it is not what we have done or who we are, but God's Purity of Purpose that brings us into affliction.

3. God Is Pure Because He Is Righteous.

I will fetch my knowledge from afar, and will **ascribe righteousness to my Maker** (Job 36:3).

Elihu described more of God's Purity by stating that He is Righteous. God is not only Holy and Just, He is also Righteous because of His Purity. *Righteous* means right doing, right thinking, right being.

In verse two, Elihu spoke to Job in God's place. Therefore, as verse three reveals, Elihu's Knowledge was not earthly knowledge, but Heavenly Knowledge. Elihu fetched his Knowledge from afar and therefore ascribed Righteousness unto God. Elihu maintained that God was Righteous in all His Ways. We need to be zealous and jealous to ascribe Righteousness to our Maker.

Everything God does for Christians is right. Satan cannot touch us without the Heavenly Father's permission. Satan could not touch Job until he had gained permission from God, and this is because He is Holy, Just, and Righteous. God foresaw an opportunity to purify Job and bring him up higher in Spiritual Stature.

4.   God Is Pure Because He Is Love.

Behold, **God *is* mighty, and despiseth not *any*:** *he is* mighty in strength *and* wisdom. He preserveth not the life of the wicked: but giveth right to the poor (Job 36:5,6).

Elihu revealed to Job that God is Holy, Just, and Righteous and that God is Love. "And *we have known and believed the love that God hath to us. God is love;* and he that dwelleth in love dwelleth in God, and God in him" (I John 4:16). Everything that God has done and is doing is for our good. Where love is, hate cannot exist. God is Mighty in Strength and Wisdom. Love works no ill will to his neighbor, and love casts out fear.

Elihu spoke on God's behalf and showed that the disposals of Divine Providence are all according to the Eternal Counsels of His Will and according to the Eternal Rules of Equity. God is Mighty, yet He despises not any. He humbles Himself to take notice of the affairs of the meanest of men, doing them justice and showing them kindness. Poverty and obscurity do not set any persons at a distance from the LORD's favor. He is Mighty in Strength and Wisdom, yet He does not look with contempt upon those who have but a little strength and wisdom. Likewise, when we are filled with His Wisdom and Goodness, we will not look upon anyone with scorn and disdain.

Job said that the wicked live, become old, and are mighty in power (Job 21:7). But Elihu said, "No!" God preserves not the life of the wicked so long as they expected nor with the comfort and satisfaction that He gives to His own people. The preservation of the wicked is simply reserving them for the day of wrath.

> But **after thy** hardness and impenitent **heart treasurest up unto thyself wrath** against the day of wrath and revelation of the righteous judgment of God; (Romans 2:5).

God pleads the cause of the poor; He will avenge the injured poor. God's pure Love constrains Him to deal honestly and righteously with **all** His creatures.

Heretofore, Job had been occupied with *self,* with his roarings, his murmurings, his flesh, but, at last, the time was at hand for him to gain a new vision, a new concept, a higher vision of God. God knows how to deal with us and bring us to a place of desired spiritual growth.

B.   Elihu Described God's Praise.

> But none saith, **Where *is* God my maker, who giveth songs in the night;** (Job 35:10).

This time, Elihu ministered the revelation of God's Praise to Job. Beloved, God can put praise or a song in our hearts in the night. If Job really had known God in the way that God wanted, Job would have had a song in his night season of affliction.

Do we know God sufficiently well to have a song in our hearts in the dark night season when there is no ray of light and when everything presses in against us? Praise in the night comes because we are related to God and so near to Him that we can rejoice in the midst of our suffering. In one of the Beatitudes, Jesus said, "Blessed are ye, when men shall revile you, and persecute you, and shall say all manner of evil against you falsely, for my sake." He concluded by saying, *"[R]ejoice and be exceedingly glad."* This can be done only as one moves up to know God in a higher realm of the Stature of Truth or Divine Knowledge.

Elihu solved the difficulty of Job's complaint that God did not regard the cry of the oppressed (Job 24:12) by asking Job a question that explained God's stance. "But none saith, where is God my maker?" People do not enquire after God nor seek to acquaint themselves with Him in the midst of their afflictions. Many cry out in affliction, but with a complaining cry, a wailing cry, a cry of the passion and nature of *self,* not with a humble, penitent, praying cry of grace. The Prophet Hosea repeated God's Message to the people:

> And **they have not cried unto me with their heart, when they howled upon their beds:** they assemble themselves for corn and wine, *and* **they rebel against me** (Hosea 7:14).

How can we expect God to answer and relieve us in our distress and affliction when we have not rightly sought Him? Of the many who are afflicted and oppressed, few lay hold of the good that God has planned for them through their affliction. It is lamentable that so few enquire after God, when, on the other hand, many enquire, "Where is wealth? Where is pleasure? Where is success?" May Jesus help us to cry, "Where is God, my Maker?"

God provides for our inward comfort and joy during our outward afflictions and sufferings. He gives songs of thanksgiving, praise, and joy to console and comfort us in the darkest of nights, thus enabling us to rejoice and to give thanks for all things. How great are God's Mercies to us, even in affliction and suffering.

Job had not learned to rejoice and give thanks in all things, but Elihu, the mediator, led him to an higher understanding of God's Will in offering praise and thanksgiving in the night season.

C.   Elihu Described God's Power.

God is a powerful God — Mighty in Power and Strength. When we truly realize Who God really is, a fear and reverence is generated in us. We need to get our eyes on Him and become acquainted with God Almighty.

God's Power has all the following attributes:

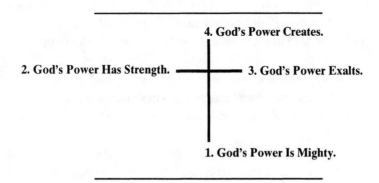

1.   God's Power Is Mighty.

Behold, **God** *is* **mighty,** and despiseth not *any*: *he is* mighty in strength *and* wisdom (Job 36:5).

Elihu continued to speak about God to Job. This time, he told Job about God's Mighty Power. It is unfathomable to conceive fully God's Mighty Power. We should be afraid to lift up our voices against a brother, a sister, a neighbor, or to make complaints against our circumstances and situations. We should be afraid to question or to doubt God. God opens our ears to discipline (Job 6:10).

If men are mighty, they usually look with contempt and disdain upon those who are not of great distinction, but this is not true with God, Who, with all His infinite Might and Power, looks upon all His Creation with love and compassion.

2. God's Power Has Strength.

He delivereth the poor in his affliction, and openeth
their ears in oppression (Job 36:15).

Will he esteem thy riches? *no,* **not gold, nor all the
forces of strength** (Job 36:19).

God is Mighty and powerful in Strength. In every circumstance,
He gives us the power and strength to abide in the occasion. The
Apostle Paul, in First Corinthians 10:10, said: *"Neither murmur ye,
as some of them also murmured,* and were destroyed of the
destroyer."* The way of escape is found in the Power of His Strength.

Elihu revealed more closely what God would have done for
Job through His great Strength, if Job had humbled himself in his
affliction.

God has Strength to deliver the poor in spirit; He looks with
tenderness upon broken and contrite hearts. He opens their ears
and makes them hear joy and gladness; He makes them hear
songs of deliverance, even in their afflictions and oppressions. In
the ears of the afflicted, God speaks good and comfortable
words for the encouragement of their faith and patience and for
the silencing of their fears and the balancing of their grief. God is
powerful in Strength to bring us through afflictions and sufferings of this present time.

Elihu's words stirred Job's heart to have faith in God's Strength.

3. God's Power Exalts.

Behold, **God exalteth by his power:** who teacheth like
him? (Job 36:22).

God has Power to lift up or pull down whatever and whomever
He pleases. Therefore, it does not behoove us to contend with the
Almighty God. The more we magnify and exalt God, the more we

humble ourselves and abase ourselves before Him. Who teaches as He does? It is absurd for us to think that we can instruct the One Who is the Fountainhead of all Wisdom, Truth, Knowledge, Understanding, and Instruction. Trying to teach God would be like our lighting a candle to compete with the sun. The great King of Kings teaches His subjects with great Authority and convincing evidence and with great condescension and compassion; none is like unto Him in exalting Power and Knowledge.

God is exalted above all; He alone has the Power of real Exaltation. He is powerful to put us down low or lift us up as He sees fit. We should humble ourselves to the size of a little worm and look up in awe and reverence at the Wonder of God Almighty and be grateful for His Mercy.

If Job, and we, too, had as much humility as we should, we would become humble before God and acknowledge that we are sinners saved by Grace who deserve the punishment of Hell. Therefore, anything that God sees fit to put on us is better than we deserve. When bitter experiences cross our pathway, we need to become humble, to get on our knees, and to say, "LORD, I don't deserve anything." Pride always says that we deserve more.

We all were sinners at birth, Hell-bound for all Eternity, in pain and suffering, but our Father sent His Son to lift us out of our poor, miserable condition and to save our souls. He puts us in the Crucified Way to bear a little suffering for a while; then, He rewards us for it. What a bargain!

We deserve suffering for all Eternity, but He redeems us, asks us to bear the Cross for a little suffering on Earth, then pays us for it. Still, we complain. What miserable creatures we are!

Although God has the Power of Exaltation, we often prefer man's exaltation to God's Exaltation. God's way is for us to humble ourselves — to get low before Him so that He might exalt us in due season. God is absolutely Sovereign and exalts by His own Power and not by another.

4. God's Power Creates.

God has All Power over His Creation; He controls it and rules it.

Elihu continued to unveil God's great and high Thoughts, in order to persuade Job into a cheerful submission to God's Authority and Power. He gave instances of God's Wisdom, Power, and Sovereign Dominion in the works of nature. For example, God rules over the rain, causing it to come down and distill in small drops. He waters the Earth, which He once drowned with rain. After the rain, He rules over the light, sending forth the sun's clear, shining rays that reach deep into the sea, thus drawing fresh vapors, fresh recruits of moisture for the clouds. How infinite is His Power!

D. Elihu Described God's Possessions.

God sent Jesus Christ to Earth to reveal a perfect picture of Himself. *"For in Him dwelleth all the fulness of the Godhead bodily."* The more we grow in Jesus Christ's Spiritual Stature, the more we will know Who God is, what His Nature is like, and what His Possessions are.

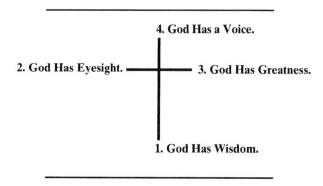

1.   God Has Wisdom.

Who teacheth us more than the beasts of the earth, and maketh us wiser than the fowls of heaven? (Job 35:11).

This verse portrays God's Wisdom and Knowledge. God possesses Wisdom. Also in parts of Job 36, verses four and five, reference is made to the Wisdom and Knowledge of God: "[T]hat that is perfect in *knowledge,*" and "[H]e is mighty in strength and *wisdom.*" In His Wisdom, God teaches man more than the beasts. God, in His Wisdom, has endued man with more noble powers and faculties than beasts, thus making man capable of receiving the excellent pleasure of God's Teaching and Wisdom.

The way we human beings murmur and complain, the doubts and questions we raise, the attitudes and dispositions we carry make God out to be ineffectual on His Throne and unable to rule anything. What a disgrace is the human race.

God still is on His Throne, ruling and reigning over the affairs of people and nations! He is Wise. In His great Wisdom, He permits proper and beneficial things to come across our pathway. The Word of God says that the nations are a drop in the bucket. Where, then, does that put us as one individual — only a small atom in that one little drop.

> Behold, **the nations *are* as a drop of a bucket,** and are counted as the small dust of the balance: behold, he taketh up the isles as a very little thing (Isaiah 40:15).

God has such infinite Wisdom that He can fashion Himself to be small enough to dwell in the heart of a man. What humility! Think of God's infinite Wisdom. Although we are so small, He plans, moves, and works in the affairs of each one of us to bring us up in His Spiritual Stature and Likeness, as we seek His Face.

2.   God Has Eyesight.

He withdraweth not his eyes from the righteous: but with kings *are they* on the throne; yea, he doth establish them for ever, and they are exalted. And if *they* be bound in fetters, *and* be holden in cords of affliction; Then he sheweth them their work, and their transgressions that they have exceeded (Job 36:7-9).

Elihu ministered to Job and showed him, step by step, Who God is and what God is like. This truly was a great revelation!

3.   God Has Greatness.

Behold, **God *is* great, and we know *him* not,** neither can the number of his years be searched out (Job 36:26).

God is so great that we cannot begin to search out all of Him. God possesses such greatness that we should be ashamed to say *we* are great or to give anyone that title. Only God is great. He is great in Power, for He is Omnipotent; He is great in Wisdom, for He is Omniscient; therefore, He is greatly to be praised. We are ignorant of what He really is. This is a good reason why we should not judge and censure His proceedings nor find fault with the things that He permits to come across our pathway. His Ways are higher than the Heavens above the Earth. He is an eternal Being, without beginning of days or duration of years; He is the Great I AM that always has been and always will be.

4.   God Has a Voice.

After it a voice roareth: **he thundereth with the voice of his excellency;** and he will not stay them when his voice is heard. **God thundereth marvellously with his voice;** great things doeth he, which we cannot comprehend (Job 37:4,5).

God possesses a Voice that will make the world tremble. His Voice is accompanied by lightning and thunder. This is why the Book of Revelation speaks of lightning and thunderings coming out of His Throne. Lightning and thunder are sensible indications of the Glory and Majesty of God; one is a witness to the eye, and the other is a witness to the ear. God does not leave man without a witness of His Greatness. The natural lightning and thunder are only a little demonstration of the Voice of the LORD. One trembles when lightning flashes across the sky and splits the clouds asunder. The Word of God is sharp and powerful, sharper than any twoedged sword, piercing even to the dividing asunder of soul and spirit and of the joints and marrow. Just as lightning rips through the sky and splits the clouds, so also will the Word of God penetrate and sever between flesh and spirit.

God's Word is powerful, like the thunder, to bring the soul into unity and harmony with Himself. In the natural realm, lightning first separates the watery clouds; then, when they roll back together, the voice of the thunder is heard. Likewise with us, if we will let the lightning of God's Word separate us from the world and the flesh, then we will hear His majestic Voice bringing us into greater Unity and Oneness of Relationship with Him.

So Elihu gave Job a revelation of God's Possessions: God possesses Wisdom, first, then Eyesight, which is followed by His Greatness and His Voice.

IV. God Had a Remedy for Job.

The fourth thing Elihu taught Job was that there was a remedy for his condition. Elihu was angry with Job's friends because they had condemned him without giving Job a remedy for his woes. Beloved, if we have no remedy for the other person, we should not condemn him.

The remedy Elihu proposed for Job's victory in his situation was as follows:

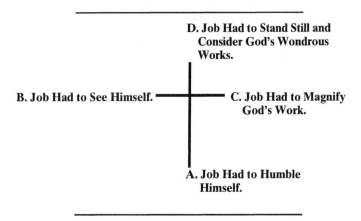

D. Job Had to Stand Still and Consider God's Wondrous Works.

B. Job Had to See Himself.

C. Job Had to Magnify God's Work.

A. Job Had to Humble Himself.

A.   Job Had to Humble Himself.

> Surely **it is meet to be said unto God, I have borne** *chastisement,* **I will not offend** *any more: That which* **I see not teach thou me: if I have done iniquity, I will do no more** (Job 34:31,32).

Elihu instructed Job according to what he should say unto affliction. Having reproved Job for his words of murmuring and complaining, he then gave Job better words to speak to God.

When we reprove, we must also be ready to instruct in the way of righteousness. The first step in remedying suffering is for us to humble ourselves. The fact that we have borne chastisement proves there is something wrong in us that needs cleansing and purifying. So we must humble ourselves before the LORD and say, "I deserve this suffering, LORD. I acknowledge that my suffering has come justly upon me; therefore, I will bear it and recognize Thy Goodness and Mercy in it." We must pray in this way: "Oh, LORD, teach me to see that which I see not. Awaken my conscience to discern, sensibly, my mistakes, failures, and ignorance as You see them." A humble soul is willing to know the *worst* about himself.

We must *humble* ourselves even *before* we see. Most of the time, we murmur, fret and strive to discern what God wants to show us about ourselves *before* we humble ourselves. Beloved, let us humble ourselves, *first;* then, we will see with enlightened eyes of understanding.

B.   Job Had to See Himself.

Job could not see *self* until he had bowed low in humility and acknowledged that God is Pure; He is Holy; He is Just; He is Righteous; He is Love.

We, too, must humble ourselves to the LORD Jesus Christ's Character and Nature, even though we cannot see wherein we are wrong, yet we know there is a purpose in our trials. We must pray for the LORD to open our eyes to the Truth; then, things will begin to happen.

The following points are the ways in which we must see ourselves:

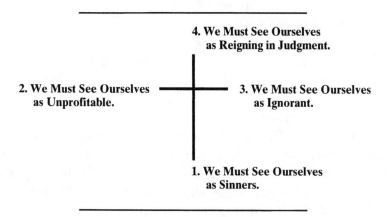

4. We Must See Ourselves as Reigning in Judgment.

2. We Must See Ourselves as Unprofitable.

3. We Must See Ourselves as Ignorant.

1. We Must See Ourselves as Sinners.

1.   We Must See Ourselves as Sinners.

Job hath spoken without knowledge, and his words *were* without wisdom. My desire *is that* Job may be tried unto the end because of his answers for wicked men. For he addeth rebellion unto his sin, he clappeth *his hands* among us, **and multiplieth his words against God** (Job 34:35-37).

Elihu, as a type of Christ, had the answer for Job and for us. We must see our flesh, our *self,* as a sinner. Paul said, "I *know* that in me [in my flesh] is no good thing." Job had spoken without Knowledge and Wisdom when he had defended himself, and he had multiplied his words against God. By not repenting of his words, he had added rebellion to his sin. It is bad enough to sin with words, but refusing to repent of them adds rebellion to the sin.

Thus, Job added rebellion to his pride and self-righteousness. Rebellion is organized, armed, open resistance to God's Governmental Power and Authority. Rebellion is a defiance and opposition to God's Headship in circumstances and situations.

The first seeds of rebellion manifest themselves in our attitudes of pulling or drawing back from that which is right, according to God's Word. Murmuring and complaining is the fruit of rebellion. When we want to do the opposite of what we are supposed to do, we may be sure rebellion is at work. We become disturbed and frustrated when situations do not go our way, and it is our pride of *self* that makes us think we know best. When we do not allow God the privilege of being on the Throne of our hearts, we are not really willing to surrender to God's Will. We must be like Job and learn that, apart from God, we are sinners and in our flesh is no good thing.

2. We Must See Ourselves as Unprofitable.

Elihu spake moreover, and said, **Thinkest thou this to be right,** *that* **thou saidst, My righteousness** *is* **more than God's?** For thou saidst, What advantage will it be unto thee? *and,* **What profit shall I have,** *if I be cleansed* **from my sin?** I will answer thee, and thy companions with thee. Look unto the heavens, and see; and behold the clouds *which* are higher than thou. If thou sinnest, what

doest thou against him? or *if* thy transgressions be multiplied, what doest thou unto him? If thou be righteous,
what givest thou him? or what receiveth he of thine
hand? Thy wickedness *may hurt* a man as thou *art*; and
thy righteousness *may profit* the son of man (Job 35:1-8).

Elihu sought to prove Job an unprofitable servant, as it were,
and, thus, cause him to justify God and not himself. Elihu pointed
out that, in effect, Job could not really do anything against God,
nor could he contribute anything to God; therefore, in truth, he
had to humble himself and acknowledge that he was unprofitable.

God is not affected by the sin nor the service of man. Man's malice is impotent; it cannot destroy God's Perfection. Man's malice
cannot dethrone God's Power nor diminish His Possessions, neither
can it disturb His Peace nor defeat His Wisdom or His Counsel.
Malice cannot rob God of His Glory. Man may hurt others with his
wickedness or help others with his righteousness, but he cannot
affect God in any way.

As we see ourselves, we learn about the unprofitableness of our
flesh. Even after we have done God's Will, there is no profit in our
flesh. We cannot take the glory for the good we do, for the LORD
put the *will* in us in the first place. He put the Power, the Word, and
the Strength in us — all we did was to use what God had given us.
Philippians 2:13 reads: "For *it is God which worketh in you* both to
will and to do of his good pleasure."

We are unprofitable because we cannot add to God's Value or
Worth or Glory, even after we have done His Will. As we do His Will,
He adds to us; He adds Spiritual Stature to us. Irrespective of how far
we have grown in God, we still cannot say, "God, you cannot get
along without me." God's Glory would not change if all Creation
ceased to exist. Whichever way we go, we cannot add anything to
God or take anything away from Him.

"Job, you are unprofitable. What can you give to God, or
what can you take away from Him? Nothing!" Thus said Elihu,
in so many words.

3. We Must See Ourselves as Ignorant.

Therefore doth Job open his mouth in vain; **he multiplieth words without knowledge** (Job 35:16).

Job multiplied his words, but without Knowledge. It was all in vain because he did not humble himself before God. To appeal to God or to acquit ourselves is useless, if we do not seek God's Knowledge and Wisdom concerning the purpose of our affliction. Elihu did not condemn Job as a hypocrite, as his friends had, but he charged him with Moses' sin of speaking unadvisedly with his mouth when his spirit was provoked. Surely, this is a lesson for us all, for what person speaks, at all times, out of God's perfect Knowledge?

Before God can give us true Knowledge, we must see our ignorance. As long as we are proud and puffed up, God cannot impart Knowledge to us.

True Knowledge and Wisdom from God is hidden from the eyes of the wise and prudent and revealed to babes. The wisdom of this world is foolishness with God Who is superior. Human reasoning or carnal wisdom are barriers to receiving true Wisdom from above. It is only as we recognize our ignorance that God can reveal His true Knowledge to us.

4. We Must See Ourselves as Reigning in Judgment.

Elihu revealed to Job what God would already have done had he humbled himself in his affliction. God would have brought him out of the straits of affliction into a broad place of plenty and blessing. But because Job tried, as it were, to usurp the Throne of God's Judgment, he fulfilled the judgment of the wicked. His words, attitude, and judgment were like the wicked; they were against God. Elihu disclosed that, for this reason, God's Wrath was stirred up and that Job was in danger of being removed with a stroke.

God is in no danger when finite man enters into judgment with Him, but when the infinite God enters into Judgment with man, then man is in danger of being removed by a stroke.

Elihu labored to instill the fear of God in Job so that he would humble himself; then, God would be able to bring him forth as pure gold from the furnace of affliction.

Job had chosen to reign in judgment and justify himself. He chose to return to his former spiritual and natural state, *before* God had permitted Satan to put his hand upon him, rather than to choose God's Judgment and go through the furnace of affliction into a greater and wealthier place, naturally and spiritually. Job had taken the throne, the judging place in his own will. He had tried to rule and to reign and to pass judgment on his situations instead of seeking God's Purpose. By humbling himself, Job would have gained his answer from God. However, due to his pride, Job chose iniquity. Iniquity means partiality. Job was partial to his former place of blessing. People had once bowed in honour and respect to him. In other words, Job wanted partiality shown to himself, thinking he deserved it. Job wanted God to change the Law of Suffering, the Law of the Crucified Way, according to his own desire.

We hate partiality when someone else gets the benefit of it, but our *self* thinks it is great when we are on the receiving end. How selfish *we* are!

Elihu informed Job that he had chosen the place of iniquity, the high seat of exaltation, rather than the low seat of affliction and humility. Job murmured and complained when God's righteous Judgment placed him in the sieve of affliction so that he might learn more of God's precious Humility. That was the wrong choice. Affliction means to abase self, to chasten self, to humble self. How blessed we are to get alone with Jesus Christ and let Him be our Elihu to teach us to see ourselves as we really are.

Elihu's remedy for Job was for him to humble himself and to see himself as a sinner, as unprofitable, as ignorant, and, lastly, to see himself reigning in judgment as he chose iniquity in place of God's righteous Judgment.

C. Job Had to Magnify God's Work.

Remember that thou magnify his work, which men behold (Job 36:24).

Elihu constrained Job to magnify God's illustrious Works. When in affliction, the next step to victory is to magnify God's *Work*. To magnify is to build up and to enlarge in one's eyes. Obviously, Job was prone to esteem things lightly and thereby belittle the things of God.

Also, God told Israel that she remembered not nor did she magnify the LORD nor did she keep the things of the LORD before her eyes. Israel forgot God until she was afflicted, time and time again.

Whichever way we look, we see the glorious Work of God's Omnipotence, whether we look to the Heavens afar off, through a telescope, or more closely at the most minute work of nature, through a microscope. The eternal Power and Godhead of the Creator is clearly seen and understood by the things that are made (Romans 1:20). Therefore, man ought to magnify and extol His good and glorious Works. If we recognize and magnify God's Headship in the natural realm, it will be easier to magnify His Headship in the spiritual realm. Since God is able to create and to rule over His *visible* Creation, He surely is able to rule over His *invisible* Creation.

To gain victory, we must start magnifying God. When we find ourselves in the low place and afflicted, we must stop and begin to look back to all the things God already has done for us. We must start counting our blessings by remembering our Salvation from sin; our freely receiving the Gift of the Holy Ghost; God's leading in the affairs of our lives; and God's revealing the Truth of His Word to us. Then, we must compare this with the present light affliction we suffer, and, in this way, we will be able to obtain the right spirit toward God. Magnifying God for our past blessings will enable us to look for the good in our present afflictions.

D. Job Had to Stand Still and Consider God's Wondrous Works.

Hearken unto this, **O Job: stand still, and consider the wondrous works of God.** Dost thou know when God disposed them, and caused the light of his cloud to shine? Dost thou know the balancings of the clouds, the wondrous works of him which is perfect in knowledge? How thy garments *are* warm, when he quieteth the earth by the south *wind*? Hast thou with him spread out the sky, *which is* strong, *and* as a molten looking glass? (Job. 37:14-18).

Elihu's remedy for Job was for him to stand still and consider. He wanted Job to stop, think, meditate, and heed.

What we *hear* is not likely to profit us unless we take time to consider it carefully, to regard it attentively, to examine it, and to think about it. In order to understand, we must stop, think, meditate, and take heed to all we hear.

Elihu asked Job to consider God's wondrous Works so that he could discern his own ignorance since he was not present when God disposed His Works, nor did Job comprehend God's Wisdom that causes the light of His clouds to shine nor God's balancing of the clouds nor how the south wind brings warmth to the garments. If man would try to answer God out of his own darkness, surely he would be swallowed up.

No wonder that, after he had magnified God's Works, Elihu suggested to Job that he stand still and consider them. Elihu, as a type of Jesus Christ, Who is our Mediator or Go-between, told Job that he would be in God's stead to him. Elihu had the revelation from God and could begin to instruct Job and advise him of the remedy for his suffering.

Elihu was saying to Job that, regardless of how much wisdom he had, God would not hear him; therefore, Job had to stand still and consider or recognize WHO GOD IS. Elihu, as a mediator, a daysman, was bringing Job into contact with God, but it was up to Job to receive Elihu's revelation concerning the remedy for his affliction, which was: first, to humble himself; second, to see himself; third, to magnify God's Works; and, fourth, to stand still and consider God's Wondrous Works. All Glory belongs to God!

Chapter Four

Job's Experience With God

Job's *suffering* was just one part of His experience in his spiritual growth; he had to have a Mediator who could show him his *self* and, then, lead him to see himself in comparison to God the Creator.

Until Jesus reveals the Father to us, and the Father reveals the Son, human beings stumble around in their darkened imaginations, trying to fit God into their carnal ideas, without any true concept of Who God is. Some say God does not exist. Some say He exists only in Nature or in human minds. Some say God is not loveable, that His Word is a lot of myths, that we do not have to recognize His Son's Blood, for God judges us by how good we are.

Since the Bible is God's revelation of Himself to mankind, let us see what it tells us about Him. These are Truths that Job learned in his experience with God.

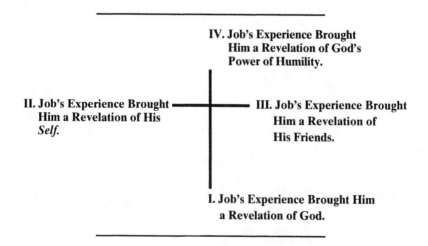

IV. Job's Experience Brought Him a Revelation of God's Power of Humility.

II. Job's Experience Brought Him a Revelation of His *Self*.

III. Job's Experience Brought Him a Revelation of His Friends.

I. Job's Experience Brought Him a Revelation of God.

I. Job's Experience Brought Him a Revelation of God.

In Job's experiences with God, he first received a revelation of Him. This is our experience, too, when we come to God and acknowledge Him as our Creator and Saviour, He always reveals Himself first; then, after we have seen Him, we are able to see ourselves. No wonder Paul said that the present suffering is not worthy to be compared to the Glory of knowing God in all the wonderful aspects of His Holy Nature. Suffering cannot be compared to the Glory of the revelation of His Word, the Glory of His Spiritual Stature within, the Glory of walking with Him, the Glory of His Presence and His Love.

Genesis, chapter one, gives the account of the creation of the Heavens and the Earth, as well as the many things on the Earth. The second chapter begins to explain the creation of man in greater detail. Man was created on the sixth day, along with the beasts of the field, the cattle, and the like.

To understand God's dealings with Job, when Job met Him Face to face, it is first necessary to study some things about God's creation of man.

> **And the LORD God formed man *of* the dust of the ground, and breathed into his nostrils the breath of life; and man became a living soul** (Genesis 2:7).

In this verse, God tells us that He made man out of the dust of the *earth*;* then, He took this little *earth* and breathed into his nostrils the Heavenly Breath of Life, thus earthly man was joined to Heavenly Life. Notice the combination of dust, which made man part of the *earth,* with the Heavenly Breath of Life, which God breathed into man's nostrils, making man a living soul. After man had sinned, God spoke to him to tell him what his life would be like from then on.

---

* B. R. Hicks, *Confirming Our Faith In What The Bible Teaches About Mankind* (Jeffersonville, Indiana; Christ Gospel Churches Int'l., Inc., 1980).

In the sweat of thy face shalt thou eat bread, till thou return unto the ground; for out of it wast thou taken: for dust thou *art*, and unto dust shalt thou return (Genesis 3:19).

Adam was a mixture of Heaven and earth. Adam's breath was a Heavenly Breath from God Himself. God took a bit of Heaven for man's breath and joined it with a bit of earth, so Adam was a special Creation all his own. This gives us a glimpse of the value and importance that God placed on man in the beginning, which far exceeded all His other Creation. It was not said of any other Creation, in the beginning, that God breathed the Breath of Life into them, only man. Since God made man so special in the beginning, man occupies a place of great importance with God. Therefore, if we take note of how well God rules and reigns over the lesser Creation, we will be well assured of His capability to rule and reign over our lives since we belong to the higher Creation — mankind.

When Job suffered, he did not take into consideration that God was ruling and reigning over his little world to bring him into a greater Breath of Life, as it were, from Heaven. Instead, he murmured, complained and asked questions in relation to his birth, his happenings; thus, he reached the erroneous conclusion that the LORD was not dealing fairly with him. Job enumerated his kind works, including his visiting widows, orphans, and the poor and needy. He was such a great one, and God had let all this suffering come on him. Why? God was testing Job's faith in His Ability to rule over the little world (dust and Heaven) that God had created in him. Actually, Job was accusing God's Judgment and His Ability to rule the world He had created.

In a dispute, it always is important to have the last word. Job's friends finally yielded to Job; then, Job yielded to Elihu; then, Elihu yielded to God. Elihu prepared the Way for the LORD to work with Job by humbling and mortifying him. This should be the office and purpose of all ministers: to prepare the way of the LORD.

God answered Job out of the whirlwind to prove to him how mighty and powerful were His Words. Even in the noise of the whirlwind, His Words were perfectly audible and clear. God designed His discourse to humble Job and to cause him to repent of all his critical expressions of God's divine dealings with him. This He did by calling on Job to compare God's Eternity with Job's time and God's Omnipotence with Job's importance. God gave Job particular instances and proofs of Job's inability to contend with Him because of Job's weakness and ignorance.

God reminded Job that, by the words of His Wisdom and Knowledge, He had created the Earth and the Heavens and that He had ruled over them very well, thus proving that He was capable of ruling over Job's personal world. The big world of God's Creation is of less importance to God than the living soul implanted within man's little world. The world will pass away, but the soul of man will not pass away; it will live on forever and ever.

Beloved, when we murmur, complain, and fret against God, we do not know WHO HE IS. What a revelation! Once we understand this Truth, it will cause us to understand Job and how God's Spirit dealt with him, which is covered in the following points.

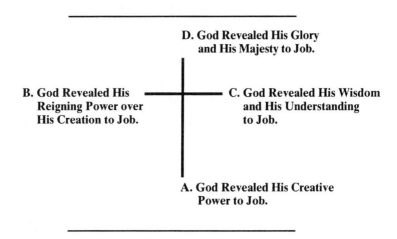

D. God Revealed His Glory
and His Majesty to Job.

B. God Revealed His
Reigning Power over
His Creation to Job.

C. God Revealed His Wisdom
and His Understanding
to Job.

A. God Revealed His Creative
Power to Job.

A.   God Revealed His Creative Power to Job.

The first thing that God dealt with in His experience with Job was God's comparison of His Creative Power with Job's inability to create. God showed Job His Reigning Power over the rest of Creation.

If God is able to create, then He also is able to rule and reign over what He has created. He takes care of the animals, and they do not have immortal souls. How much more, then, will God take care of man who has a living, immortal soul?

Next, God showed Job His Wisdom and Understanding and compared Job's wisdom to His Wisdom. Finally, God showed Job His Glory and Majesty. When God had finished revealing Himself, Job felt his smallness and nothingness before God.

God revealed Himself to Job through His Creative Power.

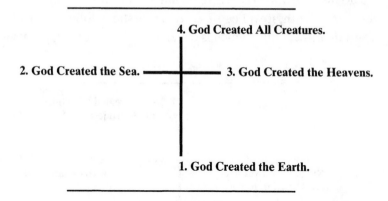

4. God Created All Creatures.

2. God Created the Sea. ———————— **3. God Created the Heavens.**

1. God Created the Earth.

1.   God Created the Earth.

The following Stature of Truth shows what God revealed of His creation of the Earth, which is where God began in His revelation to Job of His Creative Power.

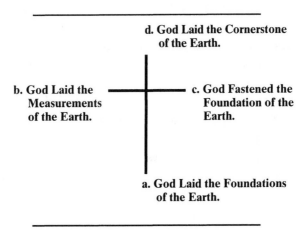

d. God Laid the Cornerstone
of the Earth.

b. God Laid the
Measurements
of the Earth.

c. God Fastened the
Foundation of the
Earth.

a. God Laid the Foundations
of the Earth.

a.   God Laid the Foundations of the Earth.

Where wast thou when **I laid the foundations of the earth?** declare, if thou hast understanding (Job 38:4).

God humbled Job by showing him his ignorance concerning the Earth that was so finely formed with such great exactness, admirable symmetry, and proportions of all its parts so that man stands in awe of its existence.

Job had made a name for himself in the East because of his wise counsels, yet he had no Understanding nor Knowledge of how God, in His great Glory and Majesty, had laid the *foundations* of the Earth.

The Earth has foundations that were laid by the Word of God. Job was ruling his own little world, his own *earth,* his own *heaven,* saying, in essence, that, according to Job's judgment, God was out of orbit since He was unfair and unjust in allowing sufferings and heartaches to come Job's way.

The revelation of God's great Creative Power should encourage us to trust in Him on all occasions and to be aware of our own contemptibleness and meanness.

b. God Laid the Measurements of the Earth.

Who hath laid the measures thereof, if thou knowest?
or who hath stretched the line upon it? (Job 38:5).

The Earth has measurements, as well as foundations. If we can perceive in ourselves the bigness, the vastness of the Earth and, then, compare that to our little world, our little earth, we will receive a revelation of God's great Creative Power. God said to Job: "Declare if you know so much. Who measured the Earth to the most minute detail without a flaw or discrepancy? Wast thou the architect that formed and fashioned it? Didst thou draw the dimensions by rule?"

c. God Fastened the Foundations of the Earth.

Whereupon are the foundations thereof fastened?...
(Job 38:6).

God was asking Job this question: "What about the fasteners, Job? What holds the Earth in place? To what is the Earth fastened?" No wonder Job became speechless in a hurry. Although the Earth is hung on nothing, it is established by the invisible Word of God so that it cannot be moved.

God, in His great Creative Power, put all the universe together. Surely, since God can rule and reign over His Creative Works, He can rule over His divine providence in our lives.

d. God Laid the Cornerstone of the Earth.

...or who laid the corner stone thereof? (Job 38:6).

The Earth has a cornerstone. There are four things that God talked about to Job in connection with the Earth: its foundations, its measurements, its fasteners, and its cornerstone.

God asked Job the location of the cornerstone that holds the Earth so that it might not fall asunder. We cannot find fault with God's Creative Power, neither should we criticize the things that He sees fit to bring across our pathway, even if they are sorrows and sufferings. If Job were so mature, surely he could repeat the songs of joy and praise that were sung by the Angels when God, in His great Creative Power, laid the foundations of the Earth.

2. God Created the Sea.

After God had given Job this revelation of the mysteries of the Earth and His Creating Power, He then unveiled His Creative Power through his formation of the sea.

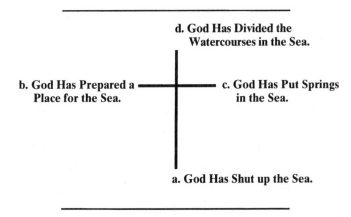

d. God Has Divided the Watercourses in the Sea.

b. God Has Prepared a Place for the Sea.

c. God Has Put Springs in the Sea.

a. God Has Shut up the Sea.

a. God Has Shut up the Sea.

Or **who shut up the sea with doors, when it brake forth,** *as if* it had issued out of the womb? When I made the cloud the garment thereof, and thick darkness a swaddlingband for it, (Job 38:8,9).

God compared the sea to a newborn babe issuing forth from the womb. In Job 38:9, God dressed the baby with clouds; He swaddled it with His thick darkness. These are His hidden mysteries to keep the sea in shape. The sea is shut up like a newborn babe in its bed, thus it is limited to its appointed place.

God knew how to hollow out the Earth and make a baby bed for the sea; then, He clothed it with clouds and wrapped it in swaddling bands that are distant and remote shores.

God was saying to Job, in so many words, "Look, as a nurse swaddles a newborn babe, I easily manage the great raging seas with their violence of tides and their strong waves and billows."

b. God Has Prepared a Place for the Sea.

And brake up for it my decreed *place*, and set bars and doors, And said, **Hitherto shalt thou come, but no further:** and here shall thy proud waves be stayed? (Job 38:10,11).

God gave the sea a prepared place to live. Valleys were sunk deep enough for it in the Earth. He prepared a cradle and set bars and doors around the cradle. He gave a command to the sea concerning its limitations. Although the sea is a vast body and although its motions are extremely violent, yet God has it under control. His Word keeps the sea under control. He restrains the tides and keeps them under control, keeping the sea inside its prepared place.

Again, God challenged Job: "With all your knowledge, Job, tell me all about the sea. If you can take care of your little *earth*, then you can tell me about this great sea."

c. God Has Put Springs in the Sea.

Hast thou entered into the springs of the sea? or hast thou walked in the search of the depth? (Job 38:16).

God asked him another question: "Job, what do you know about this mystery? Have you been there? Tell me all about the springs in the sea."

We, too, are mystified about God's Creation. The sun continually draws up vapor out of the sea, yet the sea never diminishes, and the rivers flowing into the sea do not overflow it. God has so provided and created the world's water supply that it moves and works to perfection, constantly keeping nature in balance. God has created springs within the sea to feed it just enough water to keep it in the same bounds when vapors arise from it, yet they never empty the rivers nor overflow it.

What are the sea's springs? The Bible says that, when God sent the flood, He unstopped or opened the springs of the sea to let the waters keep coming up, as well as sending water or rain down from the skies. The Word of God says that He opened the fountains of the Deep. God has secret subterranean passages through which the waters circulate.

d.   God Has Divided the Watercourses in the Sea.

Who hath divided a watercourse for the overflowing of waters, or a way for the lightning of thunder; (Job 38:25).

Hitherto, God had put such questions to Job as were proper to convince him of his ignorance and weakness, which showed Job that he should not oppose God's wise Counsel and divine Proceedings. God has Sovereign Dominion over the waters and has appointed them their courses — from the rain that falls into the rivers and, then, flows into the sea. God provides a watercourse for the rivers to empty into the sea. Our Heavenly Father controls the water so that the sea will not overflow its shores. He directs the sunshine to draw up the water, and He opens the springs just enough to keep the sea in the boundaries set for it. *"This is the LORD's doing;* it is marvellous in our eyes" (Psalm 118:23).

God was not only speaking to Job but also to us, today, when He asked, in so many words, "Can you look into this inner *earth* that I have created and show me all these mysteries, Job?" We must join Job in admitting that we do not know very much in relation to the full Knowledge of God's Creation.

3.   God Created the Heavens.

One of the best methods to use to test people's knowledge is to ask them questions. This is why Jesus Christ frequently resorted to questioning; He wanted to test the knowledge of those around Him. If we will try ourselves with questions, similar to those God asked Job, we will have to acknowledge, quickly, that what we know is nothing compared to what we do not know.

God questioned Job's knowledge about His creation of the Heavens. He asked Job about the Heavens' Light and Darkness and the Treasure House of Heaven and the Lightning of Heaven. What did Job know about all that?

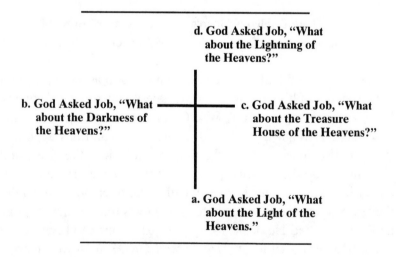

d. God Asked Job, "What about the Lightning of the Heavens?"

b. God Asked Job, "What about the Darkness of the Heavens?"

c. God Asked Job, "What about the Treasure House of the Heavens?"

a. God Asked Job, "What about the Light of the Heavens."

a.   God Asked Job, "What about the Light of the Heavens?"

Where *is* **the way** *where* **light dwelleth?** and *as for* darkness, where *is* the place thereof, That thou shouldest take
it to the bound thereof, and that thou shouldest know the
paths *to* the house thereof? Knowest thou *it*, because
thou wast then born? or *because* the number of thy days
is great?... **By what way is the light parted,** *which* **scat-
tereth the east wind upon the earth?** (Job 38:19-21,24).

God's first test of Job's knowledge of Heaven concerned its
Light. God said, "Job, if you are such a judge of your little world,
where does the light come from? What is its origin?

God is the One Who has commanded the light from Heaven to
shine, clothing the Earth with its warm garment of light — not man.
Man never has never been able to change the regular and constant
succession of light and darkness or day and night in the natural
realm. Likewise, in the spiritual realm, God orders Light and
Darkness and Day and Night for us. Therefore, we should humble
ourselves before Him and acknowledge His divine Wisdom in all the
Light and Darkness He permits, knowing that it all works together
for our good.

If we cannot rule the light and darkness in the natural realm, neither can we rule the Light and Darkness in the spiritual realm. We
cannot tell the way of light, nor how it is parted. We were not visibly
present when God spread darkness over the face of the Deep and,
then, commanded light to shine out of the darkness. Although we
may design the light of the morning or the shadows of the evening
darkness, we know not the paths of the house thereof.

We should learn to accept our spiritual days and nights, just as
we do the natural day and night, without fear or concern, because we
know God has set one against the other for our growth and development and for our rest and quiet.

b. God Asked Job, "What about the Darkness of the Heavens?"

I form the light, and create darkness; I make peace, and create evil: I the LORD do all these *things* (Isaiah 45:7).

God created darkness *and* evil. Evil and sin are two different Hebrew words. *Sin* means transgression, to miss the mark, to err against God, His Word, and His Law. The word *evil* means misery, adversity, affliction, woe. These evil things God created to be a lash on our backs because of our sin and disobedience. God, in His wise Counsel, created darkness for man's good.

Darkness, both natural and spiritual, provides a time for man to retire in quietness and rest in order to search his soul before God for hidden attitudes and dispositions that are not holy and clean. A season of Darkness will increase our joy and appreciation for the Light.

Likewise, when we were sinners and dwelt in the kingdom of Satan's darkness and, then, through faith in Jesus Christ, we were translated into His Kingdom of Light, how precious was that Light!

Light and darkness cannot dwell together in one place: when light comes, darkness leaves; when light leaves, darkness comes.

c. God Asked Job, "What about the Treasure House of the Heavens?"

Hast thou entered into the treasures of the snow? or hast thou seen the treasures of the hail, (Job 38:22).

Look at God's treasure house — the layers of snow that come down at His command. Scientists say there are no two snowflakes alike in size and design, although every snowflake is a hexagon.

God's great accumulation of snow and hail in His storehouse in the Heavens is valuable and powerful. Sometimes, God uses them to fight against His enemies, as in Joshua 10:11, when he fought against the Canaanites. Likewise, during the Tribulation Period, God will send out His treasure of hailstones in the weight of a talent (or as some have said, as large as a city block), when He contends with the world for receiving the Antichrist. God can fight effectively with snow and hail; therefore, it is great folly for man to strive against God Who is thus prepared for battle. It is better for man to make peace with God and continue in His Love rather than to contend with his Creator.

Out of whose womb came the ice? and the hoary frost of heaven, who hath gendered it? (Job 38:29).

God asked Job another barrage of questions: "Have you seen my treasure house of ice, the hoary frost of Heaven? Who gendered it? Who gave birth to it?"

Ice and frost are common things; however, this does not lesson the greatness of God's Creative Power because He formed them in His Treasure House. What a vast change transpires on the face of the Earth when God sends forth His ice and frost.

The amazing beauty of frost is something that man cannot imitate. Who besides God can clothe every leaf, every twig, and every blade of grass with crystal ice and with frost so delicate and reflective that everything has a sparkling, dazzling beauty all its own? There is nothing equal to it for breathtaking wonder.

God said, "All of these obey Me. Can you trust Me for your little world, Job? Do you not think that I am great enough to rule and reign over your little *earth?*"

d. God Asked Job, "What about the Lightning of the Heavens?"

Who hath divided a watercourse for the overflowing of waters, or **a way for the lightning of thunder;** (Job 38:25).

God has dominion over the lightning and thunder that go in the paths in which He directs them — not randomly. We need not fear God's lightning as though it were shot forth blindly, for it is sent forth according to His Command and His Will. How weak and helpless man is! He cannot command one flash of lightning to come forth. Surely, if we cannot rule over God's natural Creation, which is lesser, then we are incapable of ruling over the spiritual Creation, namely, our spirits and souls.

God questioned Job in order to make him meditate on his own nothingness and thereby give the necessary Glory to God concerning His Greatness, His Power, and His Ability to rule and reign over all His Creation, including man.

Thus, seeing that God rules over all Creation — the Light, the Darkness, the Treasure House of ice, snow, hail, frost, and the lightning — and seeing that He knows His Purpose and reason for it all, we must conclude that surely God could rule and reign over the affairs and circumstances of Job's life for his good and for God's Spirit and Glory.

4. God Created All Creatures.

In chapter thirty-nine of the Book of Job, God mentioned the wild goat, the wild ass, and the wild unicorn, as a demonstration of their wild, untamable natures. He did not describe His detailed creation of them, as He did the peacock, ostrich, horse, and behemoth, but God introduced them to Job to further convince Job of his ignorance and his lack of power to bring them under subjection.

God told Job of His creation of the Earth, the Sea, and the Heavens, first, because He created these things for services and blessings to His creatures upon the Earth. Each creature God created has a meaning. He uses some of His creatures as illustrations of the Ruling and Reigning Power of His Son Jesus Christ, such as the lion. Some of his creatures illustrate His Son Jesus Christ's Subjection and Humility, such as lambs, sheep, and the ox. Other creatures illustrate the wild, rebellious nature of man, such as the wild ass and the wild goat; while still others illustrate man's pride, such as the peacock. Some of God's creatures illustrate the wisdom of fallen Lucifer, such as the serpent. God's use of His natural creatures to illustrate abstract characteristics are almost limitless.

In His talk with Job, when referring to the creatures on Earth, God started with the peacock.

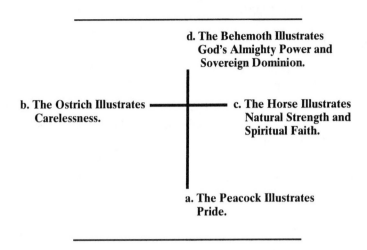

a.   **The Peacock Illustrates Pride.**

Gavest thou **the goodly wings unto the peacocks?** or
wings and feathers unto the ostrich? (Job 39:13).

The peacock with its goodly feathers is an emblem of pride as he struts and displays his fine feathers. Beautiful feathers make proud birds. However, if other birds do not envy and complain because they do not have the fine feathers of the peacock, why should we human beings envy and complain because others are clothed with garments that we cannot afford?

God invited Job to look at the way He had created the beautiful wings of the peacock. Each wing is so lovely with its uniform markings and myriad colors. God was saying to Job, "If, by my power, I created the lowly peacock with such magnificent beauty, then, through this furnace of affliction that you are experiencing, I will add more beauty to your Spiritual Stature."

b.   The Ostrich Illustrates Carelessness.

In contrast, the next creature God pointed out to Job was the ostrich, which has goodly feathers; however, it is a foolish bird "[B]ecause God hath deprived her of wisdom, neither hath he imparted to her understanding" (John 39:17). Ostrich plumes are so pretty, soft, and fluffy, having a beauty all their own. Ostriches grow these beautiful plumes from a substance God created inside of them.

Although the ostrich has beautiful wings and feathers, she is careless with her young. Dropping her eggs anywhere upon the ground, she takes no thought of caring for them, but leaves them in the sand for the sun to warm so that they will hatch. She leaves them in danger of men's feet and wild beasts. She is hardened, without natural affection for her young. Nevertheless, God, in His great Power and Mercy, oversees and preserves her eggs and brings forth her young.

God said, as it were, "Job, look, if I can do this for the foolish ostrich, how much more will I do for you in the furnace of affliction?"

We, too, are sometimes like the foolish ostrich. God gives us Living Truth from His Word, but we lay it, as it were, on the sand for anyone to trample and mar instead of clutching it to our hearts. Yet God takes care of us, who are dull and stupid, and puts His precious Treasures of Truth in us and causes us to grow beautiful spiritual "feathers," so to speak.

c.   The Horse Illustrates Natural Strength and Spiritual Faith.

Hast thou given the horse strength? hast thou clothed his neck with thunder? (John 39:19).

God said to Job, in so many words, "Have you created the horse and given it strength? Can you make him afraid?" The horse uses his strength for man, although man has not given the horse his strength. Rather, God has given the horse its strength, but He does not delight in that strength, for the Bible says, "He delighteth not in

110

the strength of the horse: he taketh not pleasure in the legs of a man" (Psalm 147:10). No creature has served man in any greater measure than the horse, which runs, draws, and carries, according to man's needs for his services. The horse has a bold, stout spirit. Even our automobile engines are measured by so many "horsepower".

God described the Horse of Faith to Job, listing sixteen of his attributes.

(1) The Horse of Faith "Has Been Given Strength" (Verse 19).

It is amazing how much strength God has given a natural horse and how much it can pull. The description here, however, goes beyond a natural horse to the spiritual Horse of Faith.

Only God, Who is the Fountainhead of all Strength and Power, can give strength. Job was shown his need to have the Horse of Faith strengthened in him so that he could entrust his little world into God's powerful Hands.

Our Horse of Faith can take us through the mud and mire of our "earth", spiritually, just as a horse does in the natural realm. The journey of this life sometimes is rough, but the Horse of Faith will carry us through.

(2) The Horse of Faith "Has His Neck Clothed with Thunder" (Verse 19).

The large flowing mane of the natural horse is a picture of the thundering power of the Horse of Faith. Thunder speaks of being shaken and brought together in great unity and power. The Horse of Faith will shake asunder the unbelief in our flesh and our will and give us victory over the world and Satan and bring us into Union with God's divine Will. How formidable is the Horse of Faith that can separate us from doubts, fears, and unbelief.

(3)   The Horse of Faith Is not "Afraid as a Grasshopper" (Verse 20).

Our flesh is like the grasshopper, fearful and ready to jump and run when the enemy approaches. We need the Horse of Faith developed in our hearts to keep us from running from our problems. We need the Horse of Faith formed in us to give us the boldness and courage to fight the many spiritual battles that must be fought in order for us to gain the precious Prize of being in the Bride of the LORD Jesus Christ.

(4)   The Horse of Faith Has Nostrils that Have Terrible Glory: "The Glory of His Nostrils Is Terrible" (Verse 20).

The expression "glory of his nostrils" goes far beyond the description of a natural horse. When a natural horse snorts about, flings up his head, and throws foam about, he is an awe-inspiring sight. However, when the Horse of Faith, whose nostrils are filled with the Glory and Majesty of God, rises in greatness of power against the enemy of our souls, he is even more formidable. He certainly will cause the enemy to stand back in fear and trembling.

(5)   The Horse of Faith "Paweth in the Valley" (Verse 21).

Paweth means to dig, to explore, to seek out, to search out. The Horse of Faith will use his strength in the valley to dig out the treasures of humility, to seek out the hidden, secret things of God.

When the Horse of Faith is formed in our hearts, through the Word of God (for faith comes by hearing and hearing by the Word of God), we will not waste time in our valley experiences or times of suffering in fearing and doubting God's Mercy and Goodness, but we will diligently seek and search for the precious Treasures of His Nature that are hidden there. The Horse of Faith assures us that all things work together for good, even our valley experiences.

112

God was showing Job that instead of riding the high horse of pride and justifying his flesh, he needed to mount the Horse of Faith in order to receive new Light and revelation in his valley experience or in his furnace of affliction.

Likewise, we often permit *self* to paw in the valley, as Job did, instead of letting our Horse of Faith come forth and dig out new Treasures and revelations of God's Word and God's Will.

(6) The Horse of Faith "Rejoiceth in His Strength" (Verse 21).

The Horse of Faith can grow and work in us when we lay hold of God's Word and let it be quickened to our hearts. The Horse of Faith brings joy and rejoicing to hearts. What joy overflows our hearts when we feel the strong support of the Horse of Faith beneath us.

(7) The Horse of Faith "Goeth to Meet Armed Men" (Verse 21).

The horse in the natural realm is fierce and furious in battle and charges with undaunted courage. Likewise, in the spiritual realm, the Horse of Faith goes forward to engage in the battle. How contrary is the flesh which wants to run from the battle and escape the Fire of suffering. What a great day when the Horse of Faith grows big enough to come forth in the battle.

(8) The Horse of Faith "Mocketh at Fear" (Verse 22).

Satan comes with his insinuations to arouse fear in our hearts, but, with contempt, the Horse of Faith scorns his feeble efforts against us. The Horse of Faith holds Satan in derision.

(9) The Horse of Faith "Is not Affrighted" (Verse 22).

When our Horse of Faith has grown sufficiently, we are not scared nor made to turn back in our spiritual walk and battle. Satan cannot terrify the Horse of Faith.

(10) The Horse of Faith "Neither Turneth Back from the Sword" (Verse 22).

Our Horse of Faith will not turn back from the sharp two-edged Sword of God's Word. He is not offended by the cutting and separations of the sharp Sword of God's Word. Neither will he turn back because of the drawn sword of the enemy because he knows that he can overcome all things of the world, the flesh, and Satan.

(11) The Horse of Faith's "Quiver Rattleth Against Him" (Verse 23).

This is the Devil's quiver of arrows of suspicion, of doubts, and of unbelief. Although the enemy rattles his quiver to try to confuse, to upset, and to disconcert us, our Horse of Faith will not retreat but will press forward and even inspire courage in the rider's heart.

(12) The Horse of Faith Has "A Glittering Spear and Shield" (Verse 23).

Satan's armor does not turn the Horse of Faith. On the contrary, he presses forward with much violence and heat against the enemy.

(13) The Horse of Faith "Swalloweth the Ground" (Verse 24).

The Horse of Faith is intensely eager to lay hold of the ground under his feet, as it were. With forceful and violent actions, he swallows the *earth* of our flesh. He also absorbs the ground of our spiritual inheritance, the Word, the full Stature of Jesus Christ.

(14) The Horse of Faith "Neither Believeth He that It Is the Sound of the Trumpet" (Verse 24).

The trumpet sound of God's Word gives the call to battle. The Horse of Faith is full of joyful eagerness to enter the battle to prove that his strength is able to gain the victory.

(15) The Horse of Faith Sayeth "Ha, Ha." (Verse 25).

The great enthusiastic zeal of the Horse of Faith makes us launch into the battle with great delight.

(16) The Horse of Faith "Smelleth the Battle Afar Off" (Verse 25).

The Horse of Faith can smell or discern the battle afar off; therefore, he is able to prepare himself in advance. We need to let our Horse of Faith grow to maturity in us, thus he will protect us from all fears and doubts that arise through sufferings and afflictions.

God was showing Job that, as He had Power to create the horse in the natural realm, He also had Power to create and exercise the Horse of Faith in Job. God was proving to Job that He was strong enough in His Power for any and every battle.

d. The Behemoth Illustrates God's Almighty Power and Sovereign Dominion.

Behold now behemoth, which I made with thee; he eateth grass as an ox. Lo now, **his strength *is* in his loins, and his force *is* in the navel of his belly.** He moveth his tail like a cedar: the sinews of his stones are wrapped together. His bones *are as* strong pieces of brass; his bones *are* like bars of iron. **He *is* the chief of the ways of God:** he that made him can make his sword to approach *unto him*. Surely the mountains bring him forth food, where all the beasts of the field play. He lieth under the shady trees, in the covert of the reed, and fens. The shady trees cover him *with* their shadow; the willows of the brook compass him about. Behold, he drinketh up a river, *and* hasteth not: he trusteth that he can draw up Jordan into his mouth. He taketh it with his eyes: *his* nose pierceth through snares (Job 40:15-24).

The record of this strange creature is found in Job, chapter forty. Bible students do not agree about what this peculiar animal was or is.

God said, in verse fifteen: "Behold, now behemoth, which I made with thee." God made this vast animal; it is the work of His Hands, the devise of His Wisdom, and the product of His Power. God was saying to Job, "I made this tremendous creature right along beside you. He eats grass as an ox, and look how strong he is. Job, consider how I care for him, yet he does not have an eternal soul like yours. How much more am I able and willing to care for you?" This great animal did not quarrel with his Creator but submissively followed God's divine Plan for his life. Should not man look at the behemoth and receive instructions from him?

The behemoth is proof and an example of God's Almighty Power and Sovereign Dominion. Let us have faith in God's Nature and Power. Since He can care so proficiently for the lower creatures, surely He can care for us.

B. God Revealed His Reigning Power over His Creation to Job.

After God had revealed His Creating Power to Job through His Creation, He began to show how He rules and reigns over all His has created. Since God was able to create the Earth, the Sea, the Heavens, and the many creatures therein, He also is able to rule and reign over them. Likewise, how much more was God able to rule and reign over Job? How foolish Job was to try to contend with the Almighty. God pointed out four things controlled by His Reigning Power.

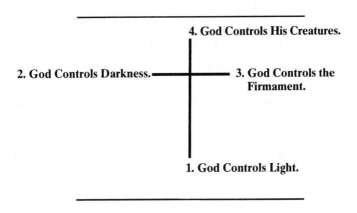

1.   God Controls Light.

Hast thou commanded the morning since thy days; *and* caused the dayspring to know his place; Job 38:12).

God created the Light, and as the Creator, He rules over Light as part of His Creation. God was asking Job this question, "Who causes the day to rise just on schedule, daily, and sees that it is never early nor late?" If God controls the natural day, surely He could order Job's day and night and rule over his soul. God was verifying to Job that He rules and reigns completely over His Creation. He is Supreme!

2.   God Controls Darkness.

Hast thou entered into the springs of the sea? or hast thou walked in the search of the depth? **Have the gates of death been opened unto thee? or hast thou seen the doors of the shadow of death?** (Job 38:16,17).

God continued provoking Job to humility and surrender by questioning him about the many things Job did not know nor understand; thus, He made Job aware of his own ignorance and nothingness. We cannot penetrate the mysteries, the Darkness, that surround the springs of the sea, the Depths, the Gates of Death, and the doors of the Shadow of Death. Yet God created the Light, and God created the Darkness; therefore, He is capable of ruling and reigning over them. God was teaching Job that He was able to rule over Job's Darkness and Death.

The Word of God says that it is appointed unto men once to die and after that the Judgment. All of us have an appointed time with Death, and it behooves us to be ready at all times. God will not be late with that appointment since He has control of that date; He rules over it. Be ready. Be prepared, for the Word of God says that it is a fearful thing to fall into the Hands of the Living God. If we have made peace with God through the LORD Jesus Christ, we will not fear the opening of the gate of Death, knowing that it is only a stepping-stone to the gate of Heaven.

3.   God Controls the Firmament.

Canst thou bind the sweet influences of Pleiades, or loose the bands of Orion? Canst thou bring forth Mazzaroth in his season? or canst thou guide Arcturus with his sons? **Knowest thou the ordinances of heaven? canst thou set the dominion thereof in the earth?** Canst thou lift up thy voice to the clouds, that abundance of waters may cover thee? Canst thou send lightnings, that they may go and say unto thee, Here we *are*? (Job 38:31-35).

By now we should be convinced, as Job was at this point, that God rules His Creation and has it under His perfect control.

God pointed Job to the firmament, to the great planets, and to the elements. He said, "Job, can you rule over all these? If not, then how can you rule your own soul, which is greater?"

Let us look at ourselves. Are we different from Job who had murmured and complained because his Father had sent him through the furnace of affliction so that he might come forth as pure gold? We, too, often murmur and complain at the furnace of afflictions in our lives until we grow in confidence toward God's Righteous Judgments, Wise Counsels, and Supreme Power.

First, God instructed Job about the firmament.

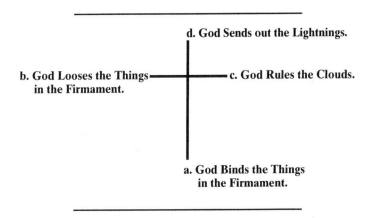

a.   God Binds the Things in the Firmament.

Canst thou bind the sweet influences of Pleiades?... (Job 38:31).

God asked, "Job, can you bind the sweet influences of Pleiades and rule over them?" Pleiades is the constellation that reputedly sheds its benign influences upon the Earth in the springtime. Yet when God pleases, He is able to bind Pleiades and make the springtime cold. It is not in man's power to order the motion of the stars, nor is he trusted with their guidance.

b.   God Looses the Things in the Firmament.

...or **loose the bands of Orion?** (Job 38:31).

"Now, Job, can you loose the great planets?" asked the LORD. Orion is that magnificent constellation that is supposed to dispense rough and unpleasing influences upon the Earth in the winter season. Yet God can, when He so desires, loose the bands of Orion and send rough and stormy weather, or He can bind Orion and make winter warm. Man cannot control nor repel the forces of spring or winter.

c.   God Rules the Clouds.

Canst thou lift up thy voice to the clouds, that abundance of waters may cover thee? (John 38:34).

God inquired, "What about the clouds, Job? Can you lift up your voice and cause them to open and pour out rain upon the Earth? Can you number them?" See what poor and indigent creatures men are? Man cannot command one shower of rain for himself on the dry, parched earth. Yet God, in the magnitude of His Wisdom, covers the Heavens with clouds and prepares rain for the Earth.

Who covereth the heaven with clouds, who prepareth rain for the earth, who maketh grass to grow upon the mountains. he giveth to the beast his food, *and* to the young ravens which cry (Psalm 147:8,9).

d.   God Sends out the Lightnings.

Canst thou send lightnings, that they may go, and say unto thee, Here we *are*? (Job 38:35).

"Notice the lightning, Job, can you rule it?" God has complete Reigning Power over His created firmament. The lightning runs God's errands and executes His desires. This truth proves His Ability to rule and reign over man's little world.

Let us be as obedient as a flash of lightning to hasten to do God's Will.

Thus, God let Job know that He rules in His firmament by binding, loosing, and by commanding the clouds and the lightning.

4.   God Controls the Creatures of the Earth.

God then pointed out to Job His Reigning Power over all His creatures that are of lesser importance to God than the soul of man, the living soul. Yet God, in His Love and Mercy, completely rules and cares for each one of His many creatures.

a.   God Controls the Lions.

Wilt thou hunt the prey for the lion? or fill the appetite of the young lions, When they couch in *their* dens, *and* abide in the covert to lie in wait? (Job 38:39,40).

God provides food for His inferior creatures, even the lions of the forest, by creating other creatures to be food for them and by giving lions the ability to hunt and seize their prey. Wherever God gives life, He also gives livelihood. God has given the lion his appetite for food and proves His All-sufficiency of His divine Providence by satisfying that appetite. Knowing this, how much more can we rest assured that He will feed and satisfy man both naturally and spiritually.

b.   God Controls the Ravens.

Who provideth for the raven his food? when his young ones cry unto God, they wander for lack of meat (Job 38:41).

As God provides for the ravenous beasts of the earth, He also provides for the ravenous birds. God continued to challenge Job by asking, "Can you provide food for the ravens and their young when they cry continually to God for food?" God is ever mindful of all the Works of His Hands. God's care of the fowls is an encouragement to us to trust Him for our daily sustenance. If we will ask, He has promised to feed us. Are we not of greater value than a raven?

c.   God Controls the Wild Goats.

Knowest thou the time when the wild goats of the rock bring forth? *or* **canst thou mark when the hinds do calve?** Canst thou number the months *that* they fulfil? or knowest thou the time when they bring forth? They bow themselves, they bring forth their young ones, they cast out their sorrows. Their young ones are in good liking, they grow up with corn; they go forth, and return not unto them (Job 39:1-4).

God showed Job what little acquaintance he had with the untamed creatures that live wild in the forests and deserts, yet God in His divine Providence cares for them.

There is an unseen force from God that causes conception among the wild animals and, then, brings forth their offspring in His time, without man's knowledge or help. God feeds, preserves, and causes them to grow to maturity.

Surely, by this point in his experience with God, God's arrows of humility were penetrating Job's heart and mind, causing him to behold his smallness before God. When we behold our smallness before God, then we will not murmur and complain about His Headship in our lives.

d.   God Controls the Wild Ass.

Who hath sent out the wild ass free? or who hath loosed the bands of the wild ass? Whose house I have made the wilderness, and the barren land his dwellings. He scorneth the multitude of the city, neither regardeth he the crying of the driver. **The range of the mountains *is* his pasture, and he searcheth after every green thing** (Job 39:5-8).

The wild ass is untamable because God has set him free. He is free from performing any service to man and has the pleasure of roaming, but the price for this liberty is the wilderness and barren land for his habitation. Not so with the tame ass who labors in the service of his master and reaps the food and shelter of his master's crib. The wild ass, having no owner, must shift for himself, yet God in His great concern for His creatures has provided green grass upon the mountains for the wild ass.

"Job, who made the ass wild? Who gave him his liberty? Who hath loosed his bands?" God asked, and Job had to confess his ignorance concerning the wild ass and his inability to tame him. But God rules over his creatures, including the wild ass.

Let us take a spiritual lesson from all of God's Creation and His Reigning Power over it to assure ourselves of His complete Ability to order and arrange the things necessary for our natural lives and for our spiritual growth and maturity in Him.

e. God Controls the Unicorn.

Will the unicorn be willing to serve thee, or abide by thy crib? **Canst thou bind the unicorn with his band in the furrow? or will he harrow the valleys after thee?** Wilt thou trust him, because his strength *is* great? or wilt thou leave thy labour to him? Wilt thou believe him, that he will bring home thy seed, and gather *it into* thy barn? (Job 39:9-12).

This great animal, which no man could tame, is now extinct. The kind of an animal the unicorn might have been is unknown, but legend says that it was similar to a rhinoceros, with a horn in the middle of its head. Anyway, it was a white animal that could not be tamed.

"Job, can you tame this wild unicorn? Can you rule him and make him act like an ox?" Thus, God challenged Job with his questions.

123

Could Job rule over the unicorn since he had set himself up as a king to pass out judgments and verdicts concerning the Almighty? If Job was unable to rule over an inferior creature, how could he then rule over himself since he was a superior creature? God again proved His Ability to reign over all His creatures — from the smallest to the greatest, from the inferior to the superior.

f.   God Controls the Hawk.

Doth the hawk fly by thy wisdom, *and* stretch her wings toward the south? (Job 39:26).

God turned to the hawk for further confirmation of His Reigning Power over His Creation. Consider the hawk, a noble bird of great strength and wisdom. The hawk is notable for its swift and strong flight, especially when winter is around the corner. The wisdom that God has given the hawk constrains it to spread its wings and steer its course toward the south, to a warmer climate, and, there, to cast forth its plumes and renew them.

"Is that due to your reigning power to give them the wisdom, Job?" God asked. We call it instinct, but it is God, His Wisdom, His Reigning Power directing these natural creatures. If He is able to rule and reign over the lesser creatures, how much more is He able to rule our lives and how much more is He concerned about the living, immortal soul He has created within each one of us.

g.   God Controls the Eagle.

Doth the eagle mount up at thy command, and make her nest on high? She dwelleth and abideth on the rock, upon the crag of the rock, and the strong place. From thence she seeketh the prey, *and* her eyes behold afar off. Her young ones also suck up blood: and where the slain *are*, there *is* she (Job 39:27-30).

The eagle is a royal bird of prey. God mentioned four particular things concerning the eagle. First, God brought the height of her flight to Job's attention.

God has given the eagle wisdom to mount to the highest rock. No other bird can soar so high, has such strong wings, or bears the powerful rays of light from the sun like the eagle. Job certainly had no power to command the eagle nor wisdom to direct her in flight.

Second, God mentioned the strength of the eagle's nest. God told Job about her building her nest in a place of safety. Her house, He said, is like a castle built on top of the rocks. No one can tamper with her young since she is out of reach of danger. High up, she has protection to raise her young and teach them to fly.

The eagle needs great heights in order to teach her little ones to fly. When the eaglets arc mature enough to leave the nest and to be on their own, the mother eagle begins to pull out the feathers and down that line the inside of the nest. She leaves the thorns on the outside of the nest to prick them, which forces them to the edge of the nest. Then, she takes the young eaglet by the beak and throws it over the mountainside. Watching carefully, she quickly swoops underneath it to catch it on her back when she sees that it is not strong enough to fly or that its strength is exhausted.

Likewise, in the spiritual realm, God has to pull out the "soft down and feathers," as it were, in our situations and circumstances and leave the briers and thorns under us in order to teach us to fly to new heights and depths in him. How we complain in the beginning when the feathers begin to fly out of the nest, and we are left with the thorns and briers. We have to learn to say, "LORD, I know that You take care of all your creatures. You reign over them. Therefore, I can trust You to rule and reign over me." The LORD Jesus Christ is ever watching and hovering around us. He never fails. Sometimes, we feel that we are headed for the bottom, but remember, underneath are His everlasting Arms to pick us up and give us strength to fly again.

Who gave the eagle wisdom to make her nest up high so that she could teach her young to fly? God gave her this wisdom, and

He can teach us to mount up with wings as eagles. They that wait upon the LORD shall renew their strength. They shall run and not be weary. They shall walk and not faint.

Third, God told Job about the eagle's farsightedness. He said that her eyes behold *afar off.* The eagle beholds her prey at a great distance; regardless of how high up she mounts, she can spot her food. The eagle is a particular enemy of the serpent. She can see a serpent on the ground from her position high above the Earth.

Likewise, when we mount up in the Heavenlies with Jesus Christ, God will let us see our spiritual enemies: the world, the flesh, and the Devil.

Fourth, God pointed out the way the eagle has of maintaining herself and her young. The eagle preys on living animals, which she seizes and tears to pieces then carries to her young ones who suck up the blood. She also preys upon dead bodies, for where the slain are, there she is.

> And **I saw an angel** standing in the sun; **and he cried with a loud voice, saying to all the fowls that fly in the midst of heaven, Come and gather yourselves together unto the supper of the great God; That ye may eat** the flesh of kings, and the flesh of captains, and the flesh of mighty men, and the flesh of horses, and of them that sit on them, and the flesh of all *men, both* free and bond, both small and great (Revelation 19:17,18).

> **For wheresoever the carcase is, there will the eagles be gathered together** (Matthew 24:28).

Thus, God displayed more of His Wisdom to Job and illustrated His Reigning Power over His Creation and individual creatures. We need to keep our eyes forever upon Jesus Christ and mount up high for a good perspective of the view below.

h.   God Controls Leviathan.

**Canst thou draw out leviathan with an hook? or his
tongue with a cord** *which* thou lettest down? **Canst thou
put an hook into his nose? or bore his jaw** through with a
thorn? (Job 41:1,2).

There is a great dispute among the learned as to whether
Leviathan was a whale or a crocodile in the natural realm. Regardless
of his natural identity, in the spiritual realm, he is a picture of fallen
Lucifer, Satan, Devil, Serpent, and Dragon. This conclusive evidence
is found in verse thirty-four which says: "He beholdeth all high things:
he is king over all the children of pride." Only fallen Lucifer can be the
king over all the children of pride. The entire forty-first chapter of the
Book of Job describes Leviathan or fallen Lucifer: Satan, Devil,
Serpent, and Dragon.*

In Job 41:2, God showed Job how unable he was to master
Leviathan, for only God can put a hook in Leviathan or fallen Lucifer.
This confirms God's Ability to reign over all His creatures in the natural world and all His creatures in the Spiritual World. Satan could
touch Job, but only as God gave him permission. When Jesus Christ
rises up with Power and Authority inside of us, He can put the hook in
fallen Lucifer (Leviathan), and cast him from our path and lead us on
in our spiritual journey with Him.

Surely, since God reigns in such a perfect, minute way over
all His creatures, He is much more able to rule over our human
souls and lives and give us the afflictions and sufferings necessary to purify us and bring us forth as pure gold.

C.   God Revealed His Wisdom and His Understanding to Job.

**Who hath put wisdom in the inward parts? or who
hath given understanding to the heart?** (Job 38:36).

---

* For a complete study on the subject of *Lucifer* see: B. R. Hicks, *Lucifer*
(Jeffersonville, Indiana; Christ Gospel Churches Int'l., Inc., 1970).

In His experience with Job, God showed Job His Creative Power and His Reigning Power. Then, He revealed to Job His Wisdom and His Understanding.

God is the Fountainhead of all Wisdom and Understanding. God has so fashioned the inward parts of man with such Wisdom, that man is made more noble and excellent than the stars of Heaven so that man shines seven times more brightly than they do. God has endowed man's heart with Understanding and the wonderful performances of thought. The powers and faculties of reason make man a living witness of God's Wisdom and Understanding. Surely, since God in His Wisdom fashioned man into a spirit, soul, and body, uniting them in such a way that is indescribable and incomprehensible, He can also order our steps and give us that which is needful and best for our spiritual advancement. So let us not pretend to be wiser than God or to understand beyond the sphere of our mortal existence or beyond the limits He has ordained for us.

God was questioning Job to enable him to see himself. "Did Wisdom and Understanding come from you? Do you really know anything about them?" God asked Job. Of course, Job did not, and neither do we if we are honest. If we have true Wisdom, God has put it in us; if we have any true Understanding, God has given it to us.

Wilt thou also disannul my judgment? wilt thou condemn me, that thou mayest be righteous? (Job 40:8).

Job had taken exception to God's Judgments, reversing them in his mind so that they appeared as erroneous and unjust. Job had said that he cried out of wrong done to him and was not heard. Such language is full of impudence and iniquity. God's Judgment must not be disannulled, for it is founded in Truth and Righteousness. If God judges that we need to pass through the furnace of affliction, then we know that it is for our good and for His Glory. Therefore, let us not disannul His Judgment and cause His Honour to suffer so that we might support our own reputation. Let us not charge God unjustly, but let us condemn ourselves and make God Righteous. When we murmur and complain, we disannul God's Righteousness and Justice.

128

Continuing through verse fourteen in chapter forty, more of the same thought is expressed. God constrained Job to meditate on His Creative Power, His Reigning Power, and His Wisdom and Understanding so that he might see God's Infiniteness and man's finiteness.

Apart from God, we are void of true Wisdom and Understanding. Therefore, it is a very proud and ignorant thing to clear ourselves and to condemn God.

D.   God Revealed His Glory and His Majesty to Job.

Deck thyself now *with* majesty and excellency; and array thyself with glory and beauty (Job 40:10).

God said to Job, "Deck yourself with Glory and Majesty if your judgment is better than mine." We cannot compete with God for Power, Beauty, or Majesty. The light of our glory and beauty in comparison to God's is like comparing the light of a glowworm to the light of the sun when it shines in its full strength. When God arrays Himself in His Glory and Majesty, the powers of Darkness quake and tremble; the Angels behold in wonder and worship; and the saints of God rejoice and leap for joy.

In dealing with Job, God caused Job to face himself, to see himself for the finite creature that he was. If Job could bring the proud low and subdue and humble the wicked by his right hand, then it would be acknowledged that he possessed glory and majesty. Certainly, by this time, Job saw that all his righteousnesses was as filthy rags and that he could not array himself with glory or beauty. He had to concede that he was not worthy to be compared to God.

II.   Job's Experience Brought Him a Revelation of His *Self.*

After God had revealed Himself: His Creation, His Reigning Power, His Wisdom and Understanding, and His Glory and Majesty, He began to reveal Job's *self* to him. Look at Job as he humbled himself and responded favorably, after he had had the wonderful revelation about God and after he had had his wonderful experience with God. He was finally convinced that he possessed none of God's attributes. Job began to humble himself under Elihu, and now, Face to face with God, he completely humbled himself and acknowledged himself to be an incompetent judge of God's Methods and Designs. The following Stature of Truth shows the ways Job humbled himself.

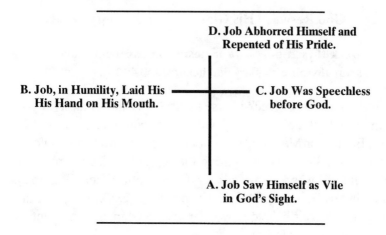

D. Job Abhorred Himself and Repented of His Pride.

B. Job, in Humility, Laid His His Hand on His Mouth.

C. Job Was Speechless before God.

A. Job Saw Himself as Vile in God's Sight.

A.   Job Saw Himself as Vile in God's Sight.

Behold, **I am vile; what shall I answer thee?...** (Job 40:4).

Job confessed, "I am vile," which means that he saw himself as small, of no account, and as good for nothing. In so many words, Job said, "LORD, I see myself; I am nothing."

Job saw himself as mean and contemptible and abominable in his own eyes. He now was sensible that he had sinned and was confounded and ashamed. Job vilified himself as much as he had formerly justified and magnified himself.

In the beginning, Job had been bold in demanding a deference with God, thinking that he could explain how just and right he was and how unfair was his suffering, but, now, he acknowledged himself to be a worm, as it were, without an answer to his Creator — a worm of vanity and vileness.

B.   Job, in Humility, Laid His Hand on His Mouth.

...I will lay mine hand upon my mouth (Job 40:4).

Job put his hand on his mouth as a bridle, as it were, to suppress all intemperate words so that they could not proceed from his mouth. Job saw that he had talked about things of which he knew nothing. Job said, "I will lay my hand upon my mouth," which means that he was vowing to say no more. As soon as he received the revelation of himself, he acknowledged his sins and retracted his statements with true repentance.

C.   Job Was Speechless before God.

Once have I spoken; but I will not answer: yea, twice; but I will proceed no further (Job 40:5).

When Job saw the error of his way and that he had been vigorously maintaining false Principles and when he was convinced that he had spoken amiss concerning God, he set about to rectify his wrong by acknowledging himself guilty and by promising not to proceed any further in his own way. Job saw his need to quit talking and to proceed no further. Those who dispute with God will sooner or later be silenced. Job finally humbled himself and confessed that he had nothing else to say; he was speechless.

After God had finished revealing Himself to Job, He then revealed Job's *self* to him. The true revelation of God, on one hand, causes us to see ourselves on the other hand.

D. Job Abhorred Himself and Repented of His Pride.

I have heard of thee by the hearing of the ear: but **now mine eye seeth thee. Wherefore I abhor** *myself*, **and repent in dust and ashes** (Job 42:5,6).

The fourth evidence of Job's humiliation was that he abhorred himself and repented. When we see God's Righteousness, we will then see our own self-righteousness and pride. Also, when we receive a revelation of God's glorious Majesty and Holiness, we will find many things to repent of in our inner self.

What caused Job to repent? Had he stolen anything? No! On the contrary, he had been a good, noble man; he had shared his substance with others. He had been a man of good works. Job repented of his self-righteousness and pride because he had thought he was more than he really was. Job repented of his complaining, his peevishness, his discontentment, and all his hasty, erroneous speeches. Job's outward expression of his inward humiliation was dust and ashes. Job's affliction had brought him to dust; now, his sins had brought him to ashes. Self-loathing is the companion to true repentance. The more we see God's Purity and Holiness, the more we see the vileness and odiousness of sin in ourselves. Thus, the more we repent in dust and ashes, the more we will abhor ourselves for offending a Just and Holy God.

Job was a believer in God; nevertheless, God put him in the furnace of affliction to purify him of his self-righteous pride. Beloved, from Genesis to Revelation, God has stretched out the Principles of the Crucified Way. God's dealings with man have never changed, and they never will.

III. Job's Experience Brought Him a Revelation of His Friends.

And it was so, that after the LORD had spoken these words unto Job, **the LORD said to Eliphaz the Temanite, My wrath is kindled against thee, and against thy two friends: for ye have not spoken of me** *the thing* *that is* **right, as my servant Job** *hath.* Therefore take unto you now seven bullocks and seven rams, and go to my servant Job, and offer up for yourselves a burnt offering; and **my servant Job shall pray for you: for him will I accept:** lest I deal with you *after your* folly, in that ye have not spoken of me *the thing which is* right, like my servant Job. So Eliphaz the Temanite and Bildad the Shuhite *and* Zophar the Naamathite went, and did according as the LORD commanded them: the LORD also accepted Job (Job 42:7-9).

After God had spoken and dealt with Job, He then dealt with Job's friends, who had bitterly censured Job as a hypocrite and as a secret sinner. However, Job was now magnified, and they were mortified!

The righteous may have their righteousness clouded with sufferings and persecutions, but, in due season, these clouds will blow away, and God will bring forth His Righteousness in His saints.

After God had humbled Job and had brought him to repentance, He bestowed honour and exaltation on him before his friends. God's pleasure with Job is expressed four times in these two verses, when He called Job His servant. God acknowledged that Job had spoken the thing that was right in that Job contended that outward prosperity was not necessarily a sign of God's Will and favor. His friends had contended that Job's affliction and sufferings proved that he was out of God's Will and that he was a sinner and a hypocrite.

Although Job spoke amiss on some things, yet God commended him for the things he spoke aright. Job was in the right, and his friends were in the wrong, yet they were at ease, and Job was in pain, which proves that God looks not on the outward appearance, but on the heart. God exalted Job to the Priesthood when He told Job to pray for his friends. God then commanded them to take their offerings to Job who would offer for them and pray for them.

God's disapproval of Job's friends is summed up in one accusation: they did not speak the thing that was right concerning God. How could they miss it? They spoke against God's Nature and

Character because they judged by Job's outward circumstances. The friends judged that God's Spirit blessed according to the standard of outward appearance, and when Job was found on the dunghill and in the ash heap, they said that God had forsaken him. They could have been no further from the Truth, as Job's circumstances later proved to be the biggest blessing in Job's life.

Job never would have continued to grow in the LORD's Spiritual Stature had it not been for the ash heap and the dunghill, for it was due to his experience of suffering that Job saw himself and became truly humble.

Job's friends claimed that God was with a person as long as he had prosperity and rich, earthly blessings. Then, when Job lost his prosperity, they said that God had forsaken him, and they accused him of being a secret sinner and hypocrite. But God became angry with these friends for their spiritual blindness.

After Job had suffered great humiliation, he gained exaltation, for God esteems that before honour comes humility. God has a way of exalting us after we have learned our lessons of humility. After Job had seen himself, abhorred himself, and had repented in dust and ashes, he was exalted before his friends.

God exalted Job in four ways: four times, He called Job His "servant." How blessed to be called a *servant,* for the servants are those who are found in the New Jerusalem — not the high, lofty, and proud. God helps us to humble ourselves to be willing to be a servant in any situation and circumstance so that we might truly be called a servant of God.

The following people were referred to as *servants* in the New Testament, which means that these were people of distinction in God's Eyes.

- Paul, *a servant of Jesus Christ* (Romans 1:1).

- Paul and Timotheus, *the servants of Jesus Christ* (Philippians 1:1).

- Paul, *a servant of God* (Titus 1:1).

- James, *a servant of God and of the Lord Jesus Christ's* (James 1:1).

- Simon Peter, a *servant and an Apostle of Jesus Christ* (II Peter 1:1).

- Jude, *the servant of Jesus Christ* (Jude 1:1).

How did God distinguish Job as a servant? He pointed out that Job was a servant to God in the way he spoke, in the way he officiated as a priest in behalf of his friends; in the way he humbled himself; and, again, in the way he spoke.

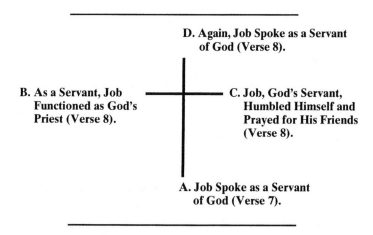

D. Again, Job Spoke as a Servant of God (Verse 8).

B. As a Servant, Job Functioned as God's Priest (Verse 8).

C. Job, God's Servant, Humbled Himself and Prayed for His Friends (Verse 8).

A. Job Spoke as a Servant of God (Verse 7).

A.   Job Spoke as a Servant of God.

And it was *so*, that after the LORD had spoken these words unto Job, **the LORD said** to Eliphaz the Temanite, My wrath is kindled against thee, and against thy two friends: for **ye have not spoken of me** *the thing that is right,* **as my servant Job** *hath* (Job 42:7).

Although Job murmured and complained in his suffering, he also did some spiritual speaking. The first thing Job spoke was this: "The LORD giveth and the LORD taketh away, blessed be the name of the LORD."

The second right thing Job spoke was this: "Though he slay me, yet will I trust Him." Job did not discern what was going on, neither did his friends, although they pretended they did.

As we walk in the Crucified Way, and every front seems stormy and troubled, it is wonderful to lie, by faith, in Jesus Christ's Arms and honestly say, "Though He slay me, yet I will trust Him and serve Him." God permits forces to oppress us in order to test us to see whether we can speak that which is right concerning Him, without murmuring or complaining.

The third right thing Job spoke was this: "I know that my redeemer liveth." Job attested that, even after skin worms had destroyed his body, yet in his flesh he would see God, which referred to the resurrection of the body. These words did not come from his friends.

The fourth right thing Job spoke was this: "When he hath tried me I shall come forth as gold." Job did not know how long he would remain in the Fire, neither did he altogether know the *why* of the Fire, but he knew that when he did come out of his trials, he was going to be as pure gold. Job had spoken that which was right! What a testimony!

B.   As a Servant, Job Functioned as God's Priest.

> Therefore take unto you now seven bullocks and seven rams, and **go to my servant Job,** and offer up for yourselves a burnt offering; and **my servant Job shall pray for you: for him will I accept: lest** I deal with you *after your* folly, in that ye have not spoken of me *the thing which is* right, like my servant Job (Job 42:8).

God continued to exalt and honour Job by saying, in so many words,"Go to my servant Job. He is a Priest, and he knows how to pray in a way that is pleasing to Me." God instructed Eliphaz, the Temanite, to take seven rams and seven bullocks and go to Job, His servant, and have him offer up a burnt offering, and Job would pray for him. When God said this, He spoke with Authority and advance Knowledge because he knew that Job would have mercy and forgive his friends, as God had had Mercy and had forgiven him.

C.   Job, God's Servant, Humbled Himself to Pray for His Friends.

God said, "My servant Job is humble now. He will pray for you." Yet it took Christ's Humility being formed in Job's heart in order for him to pray for his friends who had become enemies to him and who had persecuted him. God said, "Lest I deal with you after your folly in that ye have not spoken of me the things which are right." God often is angry with the very thing of which we are proud, and He sees the wrong in the things in which we think we have done so well. Job's friends thought they had counselled Job so well.

D.   Again, Job Spoke as a Servant of God.

Twice God honoured the speaking of His servant and exalted Job to his friends. This was a better exaltation than Job could ever have gained for himself.

Thus, we see God's revelation of Job's friends, who needed to repent, and we see, on the other hand, Job's being exalted before their faces. True revelation from God exposes *all* so that *all* may repent and be reconciled and united in affection and devotion to God and to each other.

IV. Job's Experience Brought Him a Revelation of the Power of Humility.

> **And the LORD turned the captivity of Job,** when he prayed for his friends: **also the LORD gave Job twice as much as he had before** (Job 42:10).

God's revelation to Job was how great is the Power of Humility and Patience. Although Job murmured and complained in the midst of his afflictions and sufferings, he endured and humbled himself in the end and was brought to a place of great prosperity, both naturally and spiritually. The Power of Humility will deliver us out of our distresses and sorrows and bring to us honour, comfort, and prosperity. God promises that, if we endure temptation, we shall receive a Crown of Life.

God turned Job's captivity once he had humbled himself and had prayed for those who had persecuted and falsely accused him. It was indeed a great revelation from God to Job that by praying for his friends, he would be loosed from the chains of bondage wherewith Satan had bound him. The Power of Humility would deliver him from Satan's cruel hands that had fettered him in pains, sufferings, and distresses. The Power of Humility healed Job of his sickness so that his flesh was refreshed and his mind freed from its great tumult and returned to calm and peace. The terror of his soul was lifted, his fears were silenced, and God's consolations flowed in his soul. Oh, the beautiful Power of Humility!

Job did not have this glorious experience while he was disputing with his friends, even though he was more right than they. Only when he had humbled himself and prayed for them did God's free Grace and Mercy flow into his soul. The tide was turned, and his troubles ebbed away.

Job's experience with God paralleled what Jesus taught to His Disciples when He gave them what we know as the LORD's Prayer: we have our debts forgiven as we forgive our debtors. When Job forgave his friends and prayed for them, God completed Job's remission of sins by turning his captivity.

Thus, we have seen Job's fourfold experience with God: first, he received a revelation of God; second, he received a revelation of his *self;* third, he received a revelation of his friends; and fourth, he received a revelation of the Power of Humility.

Oh, that we might learn the power of humbling ourselves before God and recognize His Ruling and Reigning Power in our lives so that we can cease our murmuring and complaining.

Chapter Five

Job's Experience in Fruitfulness

Before he could become truly fruitful spiritually, Job had to suffer the loss of his possessions and kindred and the false accusations of his friends. Then, he had to be taught by Elihu, a type of Christ, the Mediator. In his experience with God, he learned to see himself and to humble himself. Finally, he experienced fruitfulness. Job was at last ready for God to bless him with great fruitfulness, which had been God's sole Purpose in all of with affliction.

There is a striking comparison of the Spiritual Stature of Suffering to the Spiritual Stature of Fruitfulness. One must learn to be willing to forsake all in order to go on with Jesus. It means suffering to lose one's possessions, one's kindred, and one's friends and still be able to continue on with God.

Abraham also had had to forsake his kindred in obedience to God. Separation hurts, but God always makes up for it. Job suffered physically, having his body scourged with affliction, but his Spiritual Stature of Fruitfulness compensated for the things he suffered. The Apostle Paul said, in his lifetime, that his *present suffering* was not worthy to be compared with the *Glory* to be gained *in the end*.

Job reaped fruitfulness, which God bestowed on him as the result of his complete surrender to the LORD in humble confession and in growth in Spiritual Stature in the Knowledge of the LORD. The LORD recompensed Job's patience and confidence in Him. Job's wonderful increase was a special witness of God's favor and blessing upon him. Those who can suffer and retain their integrity by not turning from God are repaid with advantage and interest. When Job purified himself inwardly and prayed for his friends, he was released from his captivity of *mental and physical* suffering.

In the end, God not only exalted Job, but Job became fruitful in his lifetime. God blessed Job in four ways:

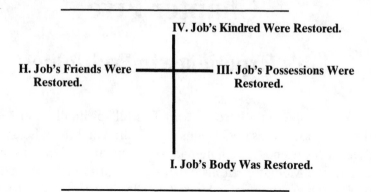

IV. Job's Kindred Were Restored.

H. Job's Friends Were Restored.

III. Job's Possessions Were Restored.

I. Job's Body Was Restored.

I.   Job's Body Was Restored.

> And the LORD turned the captivity of Job, when he prayed for his friends: also **the LORD gave Job twice as much as he had before** (Job 42:10).

When the LORD turned Job's captivity, Job's boils were healed. What a day of rejoicing that must have been for him. God restored his body and made him whole. Job was, indeed, blessed physically.

II.   Job's Friends Were Restored.

> **Then came there unto him all his brethren, and all his sisters, and all they that had been of his acquaintance before, and did eat bread with him in his house: and they bemoaned him, and comforted him** over all the evil that the LORD had brought upon him: every man also gave him a piece of money, and every one an earring of gold (Job 42:11).

All of Job's former acquaintances were restored after he had prayed for his friends. It took genuine humility to pray for his friends, and God blessed his prayer. When God's season of exaltation returned to Job, his friends, relatives, and neighbors returned to fellowship with him by eating bread with him and by bemoaning him. They sympathized with him with tender compassion and affliction. They wept over his griefs and comforted him with their expressions of affection and respect. Also, they shared their earthly wealth with Job. Perhaps they had heard how Job had sacrificed and prayed for his friends, so they desired to be included in the spiritual blessings.

However, one thing is certain, the LORD is the Head over all our friends. He can place them at a distance or bring them near, according to our good and His Glory.

III. Job's Possessions Were Restored.

So the LORD blessed the latter end of Job more than his beginning: for he had fourteen thousand sheep, and six thousand camels, and a thousand yoke of oxen, and a thousand she asses (Job 42:12).

Remember, in the beginning, Job lost all his possessions; then, God restored his possessions after he had met the condition and had humbled himself, had seen himself, and had repented. During Job's affliction, he desired that things would be as they were before, but God blessed him more than that.

"Also the LORD gave Job *twice* as much as he had before." First, Job had had double suffering from his friends. After his suffering was over, he received double blessing from God or twice as much as before. Who but God Almighty could have done that? God could not double Job's possessions until he had come through the Fire of suffering; otherwise, Job would have been lifted up in great pride and self-righteousness. Thus, the cause of righteousness would be defeated. After his trials, God could trust Job with more.

It is truly gratifying when we can understand our Heavenly Father's wise Designs, when He puts us through the Fire and brings us to the realization that His Purpose is to reveal our pride so that we can humble ourselves; then, He can bring us forth into a greater

Spiritual Stature and bless us with greater possessions, both naturally and spiritually — greater than we had before. As we grow spiritually, we will love our Heavenly Father more and more.

Job 1:3 tells about Job's wealth in the beginning of his trials; then, Job 42:12 tells about his possessions after he had gone through the Fires of testing.

Job's First Possessions	Job's Later Possessions
7,000 Sheep	Doubled to 14,000 Sheep
3,000 Camels	Doubled to 6,000 Camels
500 Yoke of Oxen	Doubled to 1,000 Yoke of Oxen
500 She Asses	Doubled to 1,000 She Asses
7 Sons	Again Bore 7 Sons
3 Daughters	Again Bore 3 Daughters

If Job was the greatest man in the East before he had lost everything, how great must he have been after God's double portion of blessing on him, following his afflictions.

IV. Job's Kindred Were Restored.

God began to restore Job's kindred after his body and his possessions and his friends had been restored to him. His most precious, prized possession was restored last, namely, his kindred. All that God had permitted Job to lose in the beginning, He restored and more too. God's storehouse of blessing is inexhaustible.

Beloved, if we are willing to suffer humiliation before our kindred, God will open the way to exalt us before them. Our kindred may despise the Crucified Way and draw back, but the day will come when God will put them in a situation where they will desire our sacrifice, as it were, just as Job's friends did. Let us put our kindred on

142

God's Altar, or in other words, let us put them in God's Hands. Let us cease worrying and continue to grow in the Spiritual Stature of Jesus Christ; then, we, like Job, will be able to pray for them and help them spiritually.

No mention is made about Job's brothers or sisters visiting him while he was on the ash heap. No doubt they were ashamed of him. In the beginning, Job cried for pity, for human understanding, for spiritual consolation, and for help. He wanted someone to comfort and console him, but Job did not receive the attention he desired because God wanted him to look unto Him for Understanding and Comfort that satisfies the longing of the heart. Thus, when we are comforted of God, we are able to comfort others with the Comfort we have received from Him. In Second Corinthians 1:4, we read these words: "Who comforteth us in all our tribulation, that we may be able to comfort them which are in trouble, by the comfort wherewith we ourselves are comforted of God."

When we are satisfied with the Comfort of God's Spirit, He will add to it the human comfort of our friends and relatives. After Job had been satisfied with God's Comfort, his friends and relatives comforted him by giving him money and gifts. If Job had not learned his great lesson of humility before God, he probably would not have received his friends' and relatives' charitable gifts.

The number of Job's children was the same as before. But if we consider that the first group was saved because Job had sacrificed for them, then they were preserved in a better place, so that, now, with his first children saved, he had a double portion of children; one group already in Paradise and the other group on Earth.

The names of his daughters were registered because the signification of them perpetuates the remembrance of God's Goodness and Blessing to Job.

A.   Job's First Daughter Was Jemima.

And **he called the name of the first, Jemima;...** (Job 42:14).

The name *Jemima* means *shining forth* and *fair of days*. Jemima was a symbol of the shining forth of the blessing and fruitfulness that God had put upon Job. Job's prosperity shone forth after his long night of dark afflictions. Jemima represented a new, bright, shining day for Job.

B.   Job's Second Daughter Was Kezia.

...and the name of the second, Kezia;... (Job 42:14).

The name *Kezia* comes from the word *cassia* and means *fragrance and surrender*. In Hebrew, the word for acacia is the same as the word for shittim wood, from which the Tabernacle was made. The cassia wood was a beautiful, indestructible wood that no insect could penetrate. It was a wonderful type of the Body of the Crucified Christ. Job had learned more about Christ, while in the Fire, and about the fragrance and durability that come out of surrender. Kezia was a living symbol of God's healing of Job's offensive boils and odors in his body and his pride and rebellion in the spiritual realm. His healing filled him with the fragrant smell of health and strength in the natural realm and with the fragrance of humility and surrender in the spiritual realm.

C.   Job's Third Daughter Was Keren-Happuch.

...and **the name of the third, Keren-happuch** (Job 42:14).

The name *Keren-happuch* means *horn of plenty, the blessing of the LORD*. The horn of plenty, used to decorate dishes, trays, and pictures, usually is filled with fruits, vegetables, or flowers, and is a symbol of abundance or plenty. God had wiped the sorrow from Job's heart and the tears from his eyes and had blessed him with great abundance, both in the natural realm and in the spiritual realm. Keren-happuch was a living symbol of this blessing.

The daughters of Job were more beautiful than all the daughters of the East. What is more beautiful than the light of a new day, the fragrance of new life and humility, and the abundance of God's Goodness and Mercy? No wonder Job gave these daughters an inheritance among their brethren, making them co-heirs.

The Fire of the furnace of affliction will not hurt us nor shorten our lives; rather, it adds to the length of our days on Earth. Sometimes, we may think we are dying when we are suffering, and we *should* die, inside, to pride and rebellion, but as we do God's Will, He will bring us up with new Strength and new Life.

Job lived 140 years after his time of affliction and saw his children to the fourth generation. He had the testimony that he died, being old and full of days. He lived until he was satisfied to leave this world. He came to a ripe maturity of age and departed, leaving a wonderful testimony and example to his posterity and to the world of the great Purposes and Designs God works in us through suffering.

Thus, we have seen the tremendous Stature of Truth concerning Job's life. First, his experience in suffering; second, his experience with Elihu, the mediator, the daysman; third, his experience with God; and, fourth, his experience in fruitfulness.

Beloved, the Stature of Truth of Job's life should be a tremendous encouragement to all of us. Nobody can escape suffering, for it comes to saint and sinner alike. However, we no longer have to fret and seek to justify ourselves, as Job did in the beginning of his suffering. Once we realize the blessings and the fruitfulness that God has purposed to give us, we can quickly humble our hearts in every circumstance of life. We can look past the visible instrument that is afflicting us; we can look past our miserable comforters and see the Plan of a Merciful and Loving God Who has permitted our lives to be touched by pain. Truly, life is a romance when we go on for God, for He has blessings hidden all along the Way to Eternal Glory. Amen.

Outline

Introduction

Chapter One:
Job's Character

I.   Job Was Perfect.
II.   Job Was Upright.
III. Job Feared God.
IV. Job Eschewed Evil.

Chapter Two:
Job's Experience With Suffering

I.   God Had Blessed Job with Many Possessions; then, He Suffered Their Complete Loss.
   A.   Satan Came before God to Accuse Job.
      1.   Satan Travelled To and Fro and Up and Down in the Earth, Looking for Christians to Accuse before God.
      2.   Satan Complained to God about Job.
   B.   God Allowed Job's Possessions to Be Touched.
      1.   The Sabeans Destroyed Job's Possessions.
      2.   The Fire of God from Heaven Destroyed More of Job's Possessions.
      3.   The Hand of the Chaldeans Destroyed Even More of Job's Possessions.
II.   Job's Kindred Were a Source of His Suffering.
A.   Job Reacted to His Suffering in Four Ways.
      1.   Job Rent His Mantle.
      2.   Job Shaved His Head.
      3.   Job Fell Down.
      4.   Job Worshipped God.

      a.   Job Acknowledged: "Naked Came I out of the Womb; Naked I Return."

      b.   Job Acknowledged: "The LORD Giveth."

      c.   Job Acknowledged: "The LORD Taketh."

      d.   Job Said, "Blessed Be the Name of the LORD."

III. Job Suffered Having His Body Afflicted.

IV. Job's Friends Caused Him Double Suffering.

    A. Job's First Physical Suffering Was Aggravated by His Having to Listen to His Friends' False Accusations.

      1.   Eliphaz Displayed His Spiritual Pride (Job, 4 and 5).

      2.   Bildad Displayed His Hypocrisy (Job 8, 9, and 10).

      3.   Zophar Displayed His Lying and Mockery (Job 11).

      4.   Eliphaz Again Displayed His Spiritual Pride (Job 15).

    B. Job Received a Second Round of Suffering at Hands His Friends' Hands.

      1.   Bildad Accused Job of Being a Sinner (Job 18).

      2.   Zophar Accused Job of Being a Hypocrite and of Being Wicked (Job 20).

      3.   Eliphaz Accused Job of Being a Hypocrite and of Being Wicked (Job22).

      4.   Bildad Accused Job of Being Proud (Job 25).

    C. In His Suffering, Job Experienced Crucifixion of His Flesh.

      1.   Job's Reaction to His Friends' Accusations Caused Him to *Pour out* His Resentment.

        a.   Job *Poured out* His Roarings in His Sufferings.

          (1)   Job Questioned "Why?"

          (2)   Job Questioned "How Long?"

          (3)   Job Surrendered His Flesh for Crucifixion.

          (4)   Job Found Delight in Overcoming.

        b.   Job *Poured out* Gall or Bitterness in His Sufferings.

        c.   Job Poured out His Tears in His Sufferings.

        d.   Job Poured out His Soul in His Sufferings.

      2.   Job's Reaction to His Friends' Accusations Caused Him to Express His Desires.

      a. Job Expressed His Desire for Understanding.

      b.   Job Expressed His Desire for a Daysman.

      c.   Job Expressed His Desire for Pity or Mercy.

      d.   Job Expressed His Desire for God.

    3.   Job's Reaction to His Friends' Accusations Caused Him to Express His Inward Impressions.

      a.   Job Felt His Friends Considered Him to Be Inferior to Them.

      b.   Job Felt His Friends Were Miserable Comforters.

    4.   Job's Reaction to His Friends' Accusations Caused Him to Express His Knowledge.

  D.   In His Suffering, Job Experienced Resurrection Power.

    1.   Job Blessed the LORD.

    2.   Job Maintained His Faith in God.

    3.   Job Received a Revelation of Jesus Christ's Resurrection Power.

    4.   Job Came Forth as Gold.

Chapter Three:
Job's Experience With Elihu

I.   Elihu's Anger Was Kindled Against Job.

II.   God Was Righteous and Just in His Dealings with Job.

  A.   Elihu Told how God Deals with Man in Dreams and Visions.

  B.   God Has a Reason for Giving Dreams and Visions.

    1.   God Sends Dreams to Withdraw Man from His Own Destructive Purposes.

    2.   God Sends Dreams to Hide Pride from Man.

    3.   God Sends Dreams to Keep the Soul from the Pit.

    4.   God Sends Dreams to Keep Life from Perishing by the Sword.

III.   Elihu Described God to Job.

  A.   Elihu Described God's Purity.

    1.   God Is Pure Because He Is Holy.

    2.   God Is Pure Because He Is Just.

      3.   God Is Pure Because He Is Righteous.

      4.   God Is Pure Because He Is Love.

  B.   Elihu Described God's Praise.

  C.   Elihu Described God's Power.

      1.   God's Power Is Mighty.

      2.   God's Power Has Strength.

      3.   God's Power Exalts.

      4.   God's Power Creates.

  D.   Elihu Described God's Possessions.

      1.   God Has Wisdom.

      2.   God Has Eyesight.

      3.   God Has Greatness.

      4.   God Has a Voice.

IV. God Had a Remedy for Job.

  A.   Job Had to Humble Himself.

  B.   Job Had to See Himself.

      1.   We Must See Ourselves as Sinners.

      2.   We Must See Ourselves as Unprofitable.

      3.   We Must See Ourselves as Ignorant.

      4.   We Must See Ourselves as Reigning in Judgment.

  C.   Job Had to Magnify God's Work.

  D.   Job Had to Stand Still and Consider God's Wondrous Works.

Chapter Four:
Job's Experience With God

I.   Job's Experience Brought Him a Revelation of God.

  A.   God Revealed His Creative Power to Job.

      1.   God Created the Earth.

          a.   God Laid the Foundations of the Earth.

          b.   God Laid the Measurements of the Earth.

          c.   God Fastened the Foundations of the Earth.

          d.   God Laid the Cornerstone of the Earth.

2. God Created the Sea.
    a. God Has Shut up the Sea.
    b. God Has Prepared a Place for the Sea.
    c. God Has Put Springs in the Sea.
    d. God Has Divided the Watercourses in the Sea.
3. God Created the Heavens.
    a. God Asked Job, "What about the Light of the Heavens?"
    b. God Asked Job, "What about the Darkness of the Heavens?"
    c. God Asked Job, "What about the Treasure House of the Heavens?"
    d. God Asked Job, "What about the Lightning of the Heavens?"
4. God Created All Creatures.
    a. The Peacock Illustrates Pride.
    b. The Ostrich Illustrates Carelessness.
    c. The Horse Illustrates Natural Strength and Spiritual Faith.
        (1) The Horse of Faith "Has Been Given Strength" (Verse 19).
        (2) The Horse of Faith "Has His Neck Clothed with Thunder" (Verse 19).
        (3) The Horse of Faith Is not "Afraid as a Grasshopper" (Verse 20).
        (4) The Horse of Faith Has Nostrils that Have Terrible Glory: "The Glory of His Nostrils Is Terrible" (Verse 20).
        (5) The Horse of Faith "Paweth in the Valley" (Verse 21).
        (6) The Horse of Faith "Rejoiceth in His Strength" (Verse 21).
        (7) The Horse of Faith "Goeth to Meet Armed Men" (Verse 21).

(8) The Horse of Faith "Mocketh at Fear" (Verse 22).

(9) The Horse of Faith "Is not Affrighted" (Verse 22).

(10) The Horse of Faith "Neither Turneth Back from the Sword" (Verse 22).

(11) The Horse of Faith's "Quiver Rattleth Against Him" (Verse 23).

(12) The Horse of Faith Has "A Glittering Spear and Shield" (Verse 23).

(13) The Horse of Faith "Swalloweth the Ground" (Verse 24).

(14) The Horse of Faith "Neither Believeth He that It Is the Sound of the Trumpet" (Verse 24).

(15) The Horse of Faith Sayeth "Ha, Ha." (Verse 25).

(16) The Horse of Faith "Smelleth the Battle Afar Off" (Verse 25).

d. The Behemoth Illustrates God's Almighty Power and Sovereign Dominion.

B. God Revealed His Reigning Power over His Creation to Job.

1. God Controls Light.
2. God Controls Darkness.
3. God Controls the Firmament.
   a. God Binds the Things in the Firmament.
   b. God Looses the Things in the Firmament.
   c. God Rules the Clouds.
   d. God Sends out the Lightnings.
4. God Controls the Creatures of the Earth.
   a. God Controls the Lions.
   b. God Controls the Ravens.
   c. God Controls the Wild Goats.
   d. God Controls the Wild Ass.

e.   God Controls the Unicorn.

f.   God Controls the Hawk.

g.   God Controls the Eagle.

h.   God Controls Leviathan.

C.   God Revealed His Wisdom and His Understanding to Job.

D.   God Revealed His Glory and His Majesty to Job.

II.   Job's Experience Brought Him a Revelation of His *Self.*

A.   Job Saw Himself as Vile in God's Sight.

B.   Job, in Humility, Laid His Hand on His Mouth.

C.   Job Was Speechless before God.

D.   Job Abhorred Himself and Repented of His Pride.

III.   Job's Experience Brought Him a Revelation of His Friends.

A.   Job Spoke as a Servant of God.

B.   As a Servant, Job Functioned as God's Priest.

C.   Job, God's Servant, Humbled Himself to Pray for His Friends.

D.   Again, Job Spoke as a Servant of God.

IV.   Job's Experience Brought Him a Revelation of the Power of Humility.

Chapter Five:
Job's Experience In Fruitfulness

I.   Job's Body Was Restored.

II.   Job's Friends Were Restored.

III.   Job's Possessions Were Restored.

IV.   Job's Kindred Were Restored.

A.   Job's First Daughter Was Jemima.

B.   Job's Second Daughter Was Kezia.

C.   Job's Third Daughter Was Keren-Happuch.